# MOSH POTATOES

# MOSH POTATOES

## RECIPES, ANECDOTES, AND MAYHEM
## FROM THE HEAVYWEIGHTS OF HEAVY METAL

### STEVE "BUCKSHOT" SEABURY

FOREWORD BY CHRIS CAFFERY

INTRODUCTION BY LUKE TOBIAS

**ATRIA** PAPERBACK
New York ✦ London ✦ Toronto ✦ Sydney

**ATRIA** PAPERBACK

Atria Paperback
A Division of Simon & Schuster, Inc.
1230 Avenue of the Americas
New York, NY 10020

Copyright © 2010 by Steve Seabury

First Atria Paperback edition November 2010

**ATRIA** PAPERBACK and colophon are trademarks of Simon & Schuster, Inc.

For information about special discounts for bulk purchases, please contact Simon & Schuster Special Sales at 1-866-506-1949 or business@simonandschuster.com.

The Simon & Schuster Speakers Bureau can bring authors to your live event. For more information or to book an event contact the Simon & Schuster Speakers Bureau at 1-866-248-3049 or visit our website at www.simonspeakers.com.

Designed by Paul Dippolito

Manufactured in the United States of America

10  9  8  7  6  5  4  3  2  1

Library of Congress Cataloging-in-Publication Data

Seabury, Steve.
    Mosh potatoes : recipes, anecdotes, and mayhem from the heavyweights of heavy metal / by Steve Seabury ; foreword by Chris Caffery ; introduction by Luke Tobias.—1st Atria paperback ed.
        p.   cm.
1.  Cookery.   2.  Rock musicians.   I.  Title.
    TX714.S422 2010
    641. 5-dc22            2010014982

ISBN 978-1-4391-8132-4 (trade pbk.)
ISBN 978-1-4391-8133-1 (ebook)

*This book is dedicated to my wife, Lisa. She is my total inspiration, and without her, life would be a mistake. I look forward to sharing charming adventures with our first daughter, Emma. This is rock 'n' roll.*

# CONTENTS

## OPENING ACTS

## HEADLINERS

## ENCORES

# EDITOR'S NOTE

**W**hen I was just a snot-nosed little punk, my Aunt La La turned me on to AC/DC's "Highway to Hell" at my grandparents' house. I was completely blown away by their music, the album cover, and the brilliant lyrics. How could you not be? Angus Young and Bon Scott are true rockers! When I grow up I want to be just like them.

During my teenage years in high school I started to play the bass guitar in my first band, Torment, and worked at various restaurants slinging pizzas, cooking up pasta, flipping burgers, and washing dishes. Playing metal with the band or cranking metal in the kitchen was a good day to me. Heavy metal music and food . . . what could be better?

Once I went to college, I realized campus food didn't taste anything like my parents' cooking. Actually it was some of the worst food I'd ever eaten. Just nasty! I quickly turned my dorm room into a prison kitchen. With the help of a coffeemaker, an electric skillet, a mini fridge, and a toaster oven, I could turn frozen pizza into something you might find in the West Village. My friends and I would buy cheap food, steal items from the mess hall on campus, and eat like kings in my dorm room. Mix some spices with a little Mad Dog 20/20, *Headbangers Ball* on MTV, and a 12-pack of cheap beer gave us a great meal.

In 1996, I packed up my one suitcase and moved to New York City. I got hired as an intern for a record company. I couldn't believe it. I'd actually found my dream job. Life was good. I told myself if you can't get signed by a record company you might as well intern for one. Most of my friends and family thought I was crazy, and maybe I was, but I ran with the opportunity and never looked back. I moved into a studio apartment in Queens with my only possessions: a TV, a stereo, a sleeping bag, my guitar, and a chair. That's it. For six months I slept on the floor like a dog and showed up to work with a smile.

I would take the subway from Penn Station to Canal Street five days a week to my office. For five bucks a day I would eat like a king. In that area I would find the most amazing Chinese food, Mexican food, and Italian food. My taste buds jumped into overdrive. Every night I would crank out to my favorite bands on tour and experience all kinds of food from every culture in the world. I love great music and I love better food!!! You can only do this in New York Rock City!

A foodie friend of mine named Rev. Ciancio writes a blog called Burger Conquest and his Glorious Pursuit of Delicious Burgers. If you are a sucker for a good burger, then this is the only site you need in your life. One night over a couple of beers, he turned me on to this gem in Chicago called Kuma's Corner. This restaurant is not only the best place to get your grub on, but it also cranks out the most awesome tunes. Chef Luke is such a badass; he names his burger recipes after some of his favorite metal bands. There is nothing better than Chef Luke's Neurosis Burger with an ice-cold beer. I knew when I was putting together this book I had to get him to write the intro. I am so glad he did.

During my time spent in Queens I got to become friends with this guitar slinger named Chris Caffery. I knew this guy could play guitar like nobody's business, but I never knew he was a chili-head. One day while we were enjoying a tasty beverage and chowing down on some bar food, he takes out of his duffle bag a spaghetti sauce jar filled with hot sauce. He cracks it open, and the smell was so heavenly. I don't know about you, but I'm a sucker for a good hot sauce. A great hot sauce can make a rubber tire taste good. Chris tells me this story about how he had been working on his sauce for some time and had just now perfected it. I had to agree with him 100 percent. It was the best hot sauce I have ever had. After washing down my meal, I had to ask him if he would like to submit a recipe for this book and to write the foreword.

Throughout the years working in the music industry I have traveled throughout the United States and Europe. I have experienced many different cultures and foods that are truly out of this world. I have been extremely lucky to work with some of the greatest bands in rock 'n' roll. I have developed amazing friendships with these artists and have learned that I'm not the only one who loves cranking out the tunes, cooking crazy meals, and eating great food.

*Mosh Potatoes* is a backstage pass into the kitchens of some of the best musicians in heavy metal music. Some of these rockers could outcook any old Top Chef.

I've personally prepared all the recipes you see here in my home. I hope you as a fellow foodie and a fan of rock 'n' roll will enjoy these as much as my wife and I do.

Beers Up!

*Steve "Buckshot" Seabury*

# FOREWORD

I was really stoked when I heard that Steve was putting this book together. I was excited that he asked me to submit a recipe. I was ecstatic and flattered when he asked me to write this foreword.

It's Thanksgiving night 2009, and I am currently traveling with the Trans-Siberian Orchestra. Even on a tour with amazing catering, I still find the urge to cook for myself. Sometimes I even make some of my classic ramen noodle recipes before I headline an arena show in front of 15,000 people. I find it both relaxing and a way for me to always remember where it was that I came from and to never take things for granted. It also stirs up some incredible memories of the last twenty-five years on the road and beyond. As a kid I was volunteered to be the family chef at a young age. My mother and father worked full-time so I was handed food and basically taught myself. It wasn't perfect every time, but that is what cooking is about. Trial and error. I learned to cook almost anything. Whether it was lasagna or stuffed shells, baked chicken or ham, soups or sauces . . . I could cook just about anything by the time I was eighteen.

As time went on and I began to travel, I would pick up recipes on the road. If I ate something I liked, I would try to find out what was in it, how it was done. During tough times I became the master of low-budget cooking for many people. Ten-dollar meals that would feed an entire band. These would be huge pots of soup, pasta meals, shepherd's pie, and many more. Sure, we had more than ten dollars, but we had to have something left over for the vodka!!! I also had the misfortune of finding out that there would be times when food was not as much fun going out as it was going in. After many bouts with food poisoning and other stomach illnesses I always seem to revert back to cooking for myself! We had a running joke on tour about a bus that one of our catering companies bought. We would say, "Poison bought them that bus . . . *food poison!*"

Inside this book you will find that many of us musicians are just as creative in the kitchen as we are in the studio. That cooking is an art. Whether it is an extravagant meal like steak and lobster or a simple appetizer like squeeze cheese and Bugles (a late-night favorite amongst myself and half-baked partners in crime), I have found that many of my friends on the road have different specialties and meals they like to share. Steve has managed to assemble many of them here in this book. I have cooked up several Thanksgiving dinners from scratch at home. Not this year, since tomorrow I have two shows, and I am excited to perform. Afterwards, I'll head back to my tour bus and make some day-after-Thanksgiving turkey sandwiches. Grab some leftover turkey and gravy, cook the Stove Top stuffing, add cole slaw, cranberry sauce, and oh yes: the instant Mosh Potatoes . . . enjoy!!!

*Chris Caffery, lead guitarist of Trans-Siberian Orchestra*

# INTRODUCTION

I've lost my mind. Clearly, I've gone off the deep end. I'm up to my arms in grease and beef, it's eight-thirty on a Saturday night, and the line is out the door and around the block. It looks like any other show you've been to. A small dark room, hundreds of people smashing up against each other, screaming at the top of their lungs, swilling beer and headbanging. Priest's "Painkiller" is blasting from the speakers in the room at full volume. I am the sous chef at Kuma's Corner in Chicago. We've been cranking out the best burgers in the country for the last few years and every night is a performance. Our kitchen is tiny, probably smaller than your kitchen at home. And whether we are debuting a new burger special like the Agenda of Swine or the Eyehategod, or hosting a listening party for a local band on the brink of success, there are two reasons we are here. Food and metal.

If you've ever been to any show that is hosted outdoors or, better, at a large-scale festival, maybe you've had the honor of being allowed backstage and having a look around. In my experience, there are a couple of things that are constants in the backstage areas of outdoor shows. Buses, beer, and grills. The latter two being, by far, the most essential. Take a walk and you'll hear the howls of camaraderie, breathe in the smoke-filled air, and smell the cornucopia of sensations rising from the smoldering coals of the grill. Burgers, steaks, ribs . . . it's summertime. Everyone is hungry, and everyone has their recipe. Their top-secret ingredient that makes *their* barbeque sauce better than everybody else's. And nine times out of ten, it's a strictly guarded secret. It's like someone took the Colonel, strapped an axe on him, got him drunk, and sent him into battle to defend the honor of the coveted eleven herbs and spices.

If you are reading this book, I'm sure you are familiar with at least some of the legends who have contributed their recipes. Whether you've stood at the front of the stage and thrown your neck out headbanging to "Into the Pit," or gotten your ass kicked moshing to "I Will Be Heard," you've never had the opportunity that you have right now. Take this chance to look into a secret society of headbanging chefs from around the world. They are opening their backstage to you.

*Chef Luke Tobias, Kuma's Corner, Chicago*

# OPENING
# ACTS

# BLACK BEAN AND CORN SALSA

## Lita Ford

This salsa is awesome with your favorite margarita and tortilla chips. I also love it in the morning with scrambled eggs and melted cheddar cheese wrapped in a flour tortilla. I love the smells of all the different ingredients. It stays fresh a long time if refrigerated and wrapped up tight. It's mouthwatering and spicy—great for parties too!

**THIS FEEDS MY WHOLE FAMILY, WITH ENOUGH FOR LEFTOVERS**

Two 15-ounce cans black beans, drained and rinsed

1 tomato, finely diced

Kernels cut from 2 ears corn

4 jalapeño chiles, seeded and finely diced

½ red onion, finely diced

¼ cup minced fresh cilantro

¼ cup fresh lime juice

1 teaspoon ground cumin

4 teaspoons olive oil

Salt

Mix together all the ingredients and chill for at least 1 hour.

Chow Down.

◆◆◆◆◆◆◆◆◆◆◆◆◆◆◆◆◆◆◆◆◆◆◆◆◆◆◆◆◆◆◆◆◆◆◆◆◆◆◆◆◆◆◆◆

# PARTY POTATOES

## Tyler Connolly, *Theory of a Deadman*

The first time I had Party Potatoes was at my wife's parents' house on Vancouver Island. Took one bite and thought, *This is the bomb!!* These go with any dish and are great as a morning hangover remedy. The only thing missing from this rock 'n' roll staple is waking up next to Giada De Laurentiis from the cooking channel. Which I obviously have done.

SERVES 6

One 3-pound bag frozen hash browns
Two 10.75-ounce cans condensed cream of mushroom soup
½ cup melted margarine
2 cups sour cream
2 cups grated cheddar cheese

Take the frozen hash browns out of the bag to thaw out a bit. Mix the soup, margarine, and sour cream in a casserole dish. Mix in hash browns and then the cheese. Bake at 350°F for 30 to 45 minutes. Eat, then partyyyyyyyyy!

◆◆◆◆◆◆◆◆◆◆◆◆◆◆◆◆◆◆◆◆◆◆◆◆◆◆◆◆◆◆◆◆◆◆◆◆◆◆◆◆◆◆◆◆◆◆◆

# ROCK 'N' ROLLY GUACAMOLE

### Jeff Pilson, *Dokken/Dio*

**T**he secret to great guacamole is really quite simple: nice, ripe, tasty avocados! You never want the other ingredients to overshadow the avocado taste, just enhance it. I don't make my guacamole very spicy. I prefer a very avocado-rich flavor, so the spice is mild. But if you do like it spicier, just add a bit of cayenne pepper, serrano chiles, or a spicier chili powder. Do enjoy. This is addictive!!

**THIS FEEDS THE BAND AND CREW FOR THE AFTER-SHOW PARTY**

3 large or 4 medium ripe Hass avocados
½ small ripe tomato
4 small green onions (scallions)
¼ to ⅓ bunch of cilantro (healthy sprigs)
½ clove garlic
½ lime
2 tablespoons LaVictoria Mild Green Taco Sauce (very important!)
1½ teaspoons chili powder
Salt and pepper

Scoop the avocados out of the shells with a spoon and save at least one or two of the pits, as we'll use them to preserve the guac when we store it.

Chop the tomato into fine bits, and avoid the watery parts with the seeds (they could add too much moisture to the guacamole and make it too runny).

Chop the green onions (use about half the stalk as well).

Chop the cilantro into small pieces, avoiding their stems (removing the leaves before you chop is easiest).

Combine the avocados, tomato, green onions, and cilantro in a bowl that has been swiped with a bit of fresh garlic (just a very mild coating). This is preferred to actually adding garlic, as that tends to be too strong.

Now squeeze the lime, not completely, just moisten the mixture mildly, and add the taco sauce.

Put the chili powder on top and begin to mash. A potato masher works well to start, then as it gets fine you can mash with a fork.

Add salt and pepper to taste. But remember that if you're serving with tortilla chips, they tend to be very salty, so you may wanna test with tortilla chips. Now pig out!!!!!

To store the guacamole, immerse the pits you put aside earlier into the mixture. Cover and refrigerate. The pits help ease the browning that tends to happen to guacamole left overnight. Should last at least another day or so.

# NACHO PIE

## Claudio and Chondra Sanchez, *Coheed and Cambria*

C ontrary to popular belief, I am not Mexican. But somewhere between the Italian and the Puerto Rican lies my inner *bandito*. I could eat Mexican food three square meals a day, and nachos would most likely be two of the three. Nachos are pretty simple to make and filling as long as you don't skimp on the cheese. My wife and I came up with this super awesome variation that we make every time I come home from the road.

**SERVES 4 TO 8**

1 tablespoon extra virgin olive oil

2 garlic cloves, finely diced

1 pound lean ground turkey

1 to 2 packets Goya Sazón con Azafrán

¾ teaspoon ground cumin

1 teaspoon chili powder

One 15-ounce can Goya red kidney beans, drained and rinsed

One 15-ounce can Goya black bean soup, liquid drained off

1 green onion (scallion), green portion finely chopped

One 15-ounce bag tortilla chips (we like multigrain, but go ahead and get crazy with it)

8 ounces grated sharp white cheddar cheese (2 cups)

8 ounces grated Jack cheese (2 cups)

**OPTIONAL GOODIES**

Pickled jalapeños (Claudio likes to buy the 100-ounce cans from wholesale stores, which last pretty much forever)

Sour cream

Salsa

Avocado, diced

✦✦✦✦✦✦✦✦✦✦✦✦✦✦✦✦✦✦✦✦✦✦✦✦✦✦✦✦✦✦✦✦✦✦✦✦✦✦✦✦✦✦✦✦✦✦✦✦

Fresh cilantro (if you're into that sort of thing)
Hot sauce

Preheat the oven to 400°F.

Heat a nonstick skillet over medium heat. Add oil and garlic, sauté for one minute, then crumble in the ground turkey. Season with 1 to 2 packets of Sazón, the cumin, and chili powder, mixing occasionally with a wooden spoon.

While the turkey cooks, heat the red beans, black beans, and remaining Sazón packet together in a large saucepan over medium heat, stirring frequently, for 8 minutes or so. When meat is browned, add the cooked beans to the skillet and stir gently together. Add the green onion to mixture.

In a 9 by 13-inch pan, arrange one layer of chips (half the bag). Cover with half the meat and bean mixture. Sprinkle with half of each cheese. Repeat with the remaining chips, meat mixture, and cheese so there are two layers. Bake for 5 to 10 minutes, until cheese is melted and bubbly.

Enjoy immediately with optional goodies, a Corona, and a funny or terrifying DVD.

# BUFFALO-STYLE BLOOMING ONION WITH 666 SAUCE

## Jesse Zuretti, *The Binary Code*

Anything with Buffalo sauce is awesome. I love it. I'll eat a Buffalo vegetable that I don't even like. If you deep-fry a mushroom and serve with Buffalo sauce I'll eat it, and I can't stand mushrooms! I stumbled across this recipe while experimenting with Buffaloing everything that I possibly could. I Buffaloed a hamburger, I Buffaloed lemongrass pot stickers, anything at all, and I just came to the conclusion that you can Buffalo anything and it'll be fantastic. The blooming onion beckoned, so I tried it out with Buffalo sauce and it ended up being a big hit. Enjoy!

**SERVES 1**

### THE ONION

1 large egg
¾ cup 2% milk
1 cup all-purpose flour
1½ teaspoons kosher salt
1½ teaspoons cayenne pepper

½ teaspoon ground black pepper
⅛ teaspoon red pepper flakes
1 large Spanish onion (¾ pound or more)
Vegetable oil, for frying

### THE SAUCE

One 12-ounce bottle Frank's Red Hot
   Sauce (or whatever you dig)
Juice of 1 lemon
1 teaspoon honey
4 tablespoons (½ stick) salted butter

1 tablespoon virgin olive oil
1 garlic clove, minced
One 16-ounce bottle Newman's Own
   Ranch Dressing (or any brand will do)

## For the onion

Beat the egg and combine it with the milk in a bowl big enough to hold the onion.

In a separate bowl, combine the flour, salt, cayenne and black peppers, and red pepper flakes. Now, slice the onion (this is the tricky part). Slice ¾ to 1 inch off the top and bottom of the onion. Remove the papery skin. Use a thin, sharp knife to cut an inch-diameter core out of the middle of the onion. Cut into "petals": Cut down through the onion as though you were cutting it in half, but *do not cut all the way through*. Turn the onion 90° and make a perpendicular cut; again do *not* cut through to the bottom. Continue making cuts, each time cutting the section in half, until you've cut the onion at least 15 times. Spread the petals out (sort of like a flower). They might keep going back, so make sure to continue to pull them apart.

Dip the onion in the milk mixture, and then coat it lightly with the flour mixture. Repeat this step. Let onion sit in the fridge for 20 minutes.

Heat oil in a deep-fryer (or a deep pot) to 325°F. Fry onion for 10 minutes, right side up. When it browns, remove it, and set it on a tray covered in paper towels.

### For the sauce

Combine the entire bottle of hot sauce, the lemon juice, and honey in a bowl.

Melt the butter (microwave is fine). Whisk the butter into the bowl of hot sauce slowly, for a good 10 minutes. Make sure the honey has dissolved into the mixture (so it's not clumpy or thick). Whisk again.

Bring a saucepan to medium-low heat. Add the olive oil. Add the garlic. Keep an eye on these guys, because they can brown, and that's not going to be a good flavor for you. Simmer for a minute or so (until fragrant).

Add the sauce mixture to the pan, and stir for 5 minutes (keep your eye on it the whole time). Pour the mixture back into the bowl. Add the bottle of Ranch Dressing. Stir liberally.

Serve the blooming onion in a large bowl or plate with deep sides. You can put a small dish inside the center of the onion, and fill with the sauce.

# HUMMUS

## Jason Becker, *Cacophony/David Lee Roth*

This is a delicious and healthy-ass dip, so you can stuff your face and not feel guilty. When I got ALS in 1989, while playing with David Lee Roth, doctors told me there was nothing I could do but die in three to five years. I had just turned twenty. I asked about diet, but they said nothing would help. I didn't believe them, so I went from a junk-food diet, consisting of McDonald's, Cool Ranch Doritos, donuts, soda, and Ho Hos, to a healthy diet. It was hard at first because everything tasted like cardboard. Then I started dating Serrana, who knew how to make delicious, healthy food. She showed me her hummus, and I tinkered with it. It was so cool to have something so delicious, yet healthy, that I could stuff my face with and not feel guilty. Whatever you dip into it, it tastes fantabulous.

### FOR 2 PEOPLE TO SNACK ON WHILE HANGING OUT

One 15.5-ounce can garbanzo beans (chickpeas)
½ cup tahini
2 teaspoons olive oil, plus more for garnish
2 garlic cloves, minced
2 tablespoons lemon juice
Salt
Paprika, for garnish
Cayenne pepper, for garnish

Pour the garbanzos into a medium saucepan with the liquid from the can. Heat gently over medium-low heat. Drain the garbanzos, but hold on to the liquid.

Combine the garbanzos, tahini, olive oil, garlic, and lemon juice in a food processor, and process to a smooth puree. Add some of the reserved liquid from the can to thin the hummus out (if it needs it). Add salt to taste. Pour onto a flat serving dish, drizzle more olive oil over the top, and sprinkle with paprika and cayenne. Serve with pita bread, veggies, or chips.

# SUMMIT SALSA

## Chris Letchford, *Scale the Summit*

**M**exican food has always been my absolute favorite style of food, which includes the almighty salsa that I personally eat daily when not on the road! I was born and raised in Texas, where all the best Tex-Mex restaurants are located. That, and the fact that both of my parents were born in South America predestined my love for spicy foods. My dad's mom was full-blooded Peruvian. When I was a little kid, whenever she made me anything, even if it was a hot dog, there were multiple jars of salsa, hot sauces, and jalapeños ready for me to grab off the table. She knew I loved hot things. Grocery stores have never carried any great, fresh salsa, so I decided to make up my own recipe to keep me covered 24/7! Enjoy!

**SERVES 4**

Two 14.5-ounce cans diced tomatoes
1 habanero chile, finely diced
4 garlic cloves, finely diced
2 green onions (scallions), chopped
Two 4-ounce cans green chiles
1 tablespoon salt

First drain the juice from each can of tomatoes. Set the tomatoes aside for later. Pour the juice into a blender (it will help blend the habanero and garlic cloves when they are pureed). Add the habanero and garlic and blend together until they form a paste. Set aside.

Next chop only the white parts of the green onions. Blend until smooth. Then add both cans of green chiles, the tomatoes, and the salt. Blend until smooth. Add the habanero and garlic paste to the mixture. Last, let chill in the fridge for 3 hours for the best taste!

◆◆◆◆◆◆◆◆◆◆◆◆◆◆◆◆◆◆◆◆◆◆◆◆◆◆◆◆◆◆◆◆◆◆◆◆◆◆◆◆◆◆◆◆◆◆◆

# GUACAMOLE

## Alex Skolnick, *Testament*

Though I have no Mexican heritage, I grew up in Northern California where *taquerias* (Mexican cafés) are as common as coffee houses in Seattle. As a result, guacamole feels like more a part of my cultural upbringing than matzo ball soup.

I threw this recipe together when I was asked to bring food to a party. I've made it countless times since, and it always seems to be a hit even though it's simple to make and can be easily adjusted to suit different tastes.

**FEEDS 6 HUNGRY METAL HEADS**

4 avocados, dark green and very ripe (the softer the better)
1 green onion (scallion), chopped
1 large tomato, seeded and diced
1 tablespoon mild green taco sauce
2 tablespoons garlic powder
1 teaspoon ground black pepper
1 teaspoon salt
1 teaspoon your favorite hot sauce, or more (optional) I like
    Blair's Death sauce and Dave's Insanity
½ lemon

Slice each avocado in half with a kitchen knife (doesn't need to be sharp), cutting around the pit. Remove pit and discard. With a large spoon, scoop contents of each half out of the skin and into a large bowl. Discard the skin. Take knife and cut avocado "meat" into as many sections as possible. Take fork and mash thoroughly.

Toss in the green onion and tomato and stir. Add the taco sauce, garlic powder, pepper, salt, and hot sauce (if using). Stir it all together. Feel free to adjust ingredients to taste. When ready, squeeze the juice from the lemon all over the top. Do not stir. Cover with plastic wrap and refrigerate. Serve cold with tortilla chips. Bueno!

◆◆◆◆◆◆◆◆◆◆◆◆◆◆◆◆◆◆◆◆◆◆◆◆◆◆◆◆◆◆◆◆◆◆◆◆◆◆◆◆◆◆◆◆◆◆◆◆◆

# BURNT BY THE SHRIMP

## Teddy Patterson, *Burnt by the Sun*

S picy, but not painfully spicy, just some damn good shrimp!

SERVES 6

3 to 6 jumbo shrimp

**SECRET BBQ SAUCE**

2 tablespoons spicy mustard (the bolder the better!)

3 tablespoons hot sauce (your favorite: Tabasco sauce, habanero, whatever you like)

1 tablespoon minced garlic

Get your favorite fresh shrimp, the bigger the better. I get them from the Co-Op in Belford, New Jersey, on the Westside! Clean them well (peel, remove veins, etc.). Stick those suckers on BBQ skewers.

Preheat the grill to medium-high.

Mix together everything for the sauce. Paint the shrimp with the sauce, grill 3 to 5 minutes on each side, continuing to apply the sauce, and when they are done, POW! You have "Burnt by the Shrimp!"

# STUFFED MUSHROOMS

## Dez, *Devildriver*

**T**his one is so easy but will please anyone who eats it.

**FEEDS 4 HUNGRY PEOPLE**

There are two ways you can do this—with bacon or spicy sausage.

You will need baby bella mushrooms (the brown kind). Hollow them out with a spoon (be careful they don't break!). Lay them open-side up on a large cookie sheet. Drizzle with olive oil.

Preheat the oven to 350°F. Fill each mushroom about a quarter full with chopped bacon or crumbled sausage. Use the parmesan cheese out of the *green* can. Use the kind you grew up with. Do not use fresh. THIS IS IMPORTANT: It won't be the same. Top each mushroom with the cheese, making a mound on each one.

Sprinkle red pepper flakes over mushrooms and a little black pepper. No salt. Bake for 15 to 20 minutes until the cheese is golden brown.

Open a bottle of red and get to eatin!

◆◆◆◆◆◆◆◆◆◆◆◆◆◆◆◆◆◆◆◆◆◆◆◆◆◆◆◆◆◆◆◆◆◆◆◆◆◆◆◆◆◆◆◆◆◆

# BLACK TUSK GRILLED SHRIMP

## Athon, *Black Tusk*

**A**lmost every weekend since the band formed, we have been gettin' together and having a barbeque. We have always been big on grilling out. One day while we were having a get-together, the food started to run short. As we raided the fridge and cabinets in the house we didn't find very much. The drawer had plenty of skewers, and there were some fresh shrimp that had been bartered for on the previous day. That day Black Tusk was like some sort of kitchen MacGyver.

**SERVES 4**

2 pounds fresh shrimp (headed, peeled, and deveined)

2 tablespoons extra virgin olive oil

¼ teaspoon each paprika, cayenne pepper, garlic powder, onion powder

Basil, salt, and black pepper

½ pound thinly sliced prosciutto, soaked in your favorite bourbon

2 green bell peppers, cut in squares

1 Vidalia onion, cut in chunks and separated

Mushroom caps

Cubed fresh pineapple (or drained canned)

1 lime

Preheat a grill to medium.

Toss shrimp in a mixture of olive oil, paprika, cayenne pepper, garlic powder, onion powder, and a pinch of basil, salt, and black pepper. Wrap a shrimp with prosciutto and place on bamboo skewers alternating with green peppers, onion, mushrooms, and pineapple.

Grill the skewers until the shrimp are firm and pink. Squeeze some lime juice over them. Take off the heat and let them rest for a couple of minutes. Serve them up on plates and drink the rest of the bourbon!

$$\blacklozenge\blacklozenge\blacklozenge\blacklozenge\blacklozenge\blacklozenge\blacklozenge\blacklozenge\blacklozenge\blacklozenge\blacklozenge\blacklozenge\blacklozenge\blacklozenge\blacklozenge\blacklozenge\blacklozenge\blacklozenge\blacklozenge\blacklozenge\blacklozenge\blacklozenge\blacklozenge\blacklozenge\blacklozenge\blacklozenge\blacklozenge\blacklozenge\blacklozenge\blacklozenge\blacklozenge\blacklozenge\blacklozenge\blacklozenge\blacklozenge\blacklozenge\blacklozenge\blacklozenge\blacklozenge\blacklozenge$$

# DIRTY JERSEY WINGS

## Anthony "Ant-$" Martini, *E.town Concrete*

This is a fairly simple recipe and chances are, even if you aren't a great cook, these will still come out bangin'.

This dish works best when accompanied by the sporting event of your choice. A sausage party entrée for sure. Dude-fest . . . no bitches allowed.

**SERVES 6**

2 to 3 pounds chicken wings
All-purpose flour
Cayenne pepper
Ground black pepper
2 large eggs
5⅓ tablespoons (⅔ stick) salted butter
Chopped garlic
Two 12-ounce bottles Frank's Red Hot Sauce (accept NO imitations!!!!)
Blue Cheese Dip (recipe follows)

Preheat the oven to 475°F.

If you really want to keep it gansta' you'll buy fresh whole chicken wings and section them yourself. Chop at the joints, leaving a drumstick and a wing (discard the tips). Mix flour with some cayenne pepper and black pepper (to taste). Beat the eggs together in a separate bowl. Dip the chicken pieces in the egg bowl, then dip in the flour bowl until evenly coated.

Place the chicken pieces on a baking sheet and bake until they are nice and golden, maybe 40 minutes or so (make sure they are cooked . . . you don't want salmonella or some shit!!!).

When the wings are finished cooking, in a saucepan, combine the butter and the garlic. Cook until melted. Pour over wings immediately. After the wings are properly coated with the savory garlic-butter goodness, pour on the Frank's Red Hot.

Serve YO!!

## BLUE CHEESE DIP

- 1 pint sour cream
- 1 tablespoon mayonnaise
- Pinch of minced fresh oregano
- White wine vinegar
- Crumbled blue cheese
- Crumbled Gorgonzola cheese
- Salt and pepper

I don't know the exact amounts of each ingredient, so you have to eyeball it, depending on how much you want. In a mixing bowl, combine the sour cream, mayo, and oregano. Add a splash of white wine vinegar until it reaches the consistency you want. Add vinegar little by little and taste as you go. Too much vinegar will screw it all up! Next, add the blue and Gorgonzola cheeses and salt and pepper to taste. Stir well. You're ready for dipping!

# VEGETABLE SOUP

## Candice and Ritchie Blackmore, *Blackmore's Knight*

This is a hearty meal that my wife and I enjoy very much. This soup combines all my favorite vegetables.

SERVES 2

5 small beef bouillon cubes
½ baking potato, peeled and sliced
2 Spanish onions, chopped
4 leeks, cut into 2-inch pieces
½ parsnip, peeled and chopped
½ turnip, peeled and chopped
2 celery stalks, chopped
¼ head cauliflower, chopped
4 Brussels sprouts, chopped
2 small heads broccoli, chopped

5 carrots, chopped
8 cherry tomatoes
10 bean sprouts
1 cup peas
Meatballs (optional; recipe follows)
2 tablespoons chopped fresh dill
Ground turmeric
Ground cinnamon
Ground ginger

Boil 2 quarts of water and add the bouillon cubes. Add the potato, onions, and leeks and cook for 5 minutes. Add the parsnip, turnip, celery, cauliflower, Brussels sprouts, broccoli, carrots, and tomatoes and cook for 5 minutes. Add the bean sprouts, peas, and meatballs (if using) and cook for 5 minutes more. Add the dill. Add a touch of turmeric, cinnamon, and ginger at the end before serving.

## MEATBALLS

½ pound ground beef
1 egg
Flavored dry bread crumbs (2 slices of bread)

Combine everything thoroughly. Roll into five balls. Fry in a nonstick skillet until brown all over and fully cooked.

‹‹‹‹‹‹‹‹‹‹‹‹‹‹‹‹‹‹‹‹‹‹‹‹‹‹‹‹‹‹‹‹‹‹‹‹‹‹‹‹‹‹‹‹‹‹‹‹

# SAUSAGE DIP

## Alex Wade and Gabe Crisp, *Whitechapel*

This is a sausage and cream cheese–based chip dip great for parties or just as a snack. It's very simple to make, requires no measurements, and is extremely delicious! Another great quality about it is you can determine the amount of heat you want in the flavor of the dip by selecting whatever sausage and Ro*tel suits you best. Most sausages and all Ro*tel come in original, mild, and hot. We make ours with hot Ro*tel and spicy sausage.

**PUT OUT AT A PARTY, IT FEEDS EVERYONE.**

8 ounces cream cheese

One 10-ounce can Ro*tel tomatoes

One 4-ounce can diced jalapeños (optional, for added heat)

One 16-ounce hot sausage

One 24-ounce bag tortilla chips (Tostitos Scoops! work great!)

Place the entire block of cream cheese in a medium bowl. Open the cans of tomatoes and jalapeños and drain both cans of all liquid. Plop the tomatoes and jalapeños in the bowl with the cream cheese.

Brown the sausage on high heat in a skillet. Break it up with a spatula or fork while you are cooking it. Cook until the sausage is brown and cooked through.

While the sausage is still hot pour it in the bowl with the cream cheese and Ro*tel mixture. The heat from the sausage will melt the cream cheese as you mix it all together. Mix thoroughly until all the cream cheese is melted and the sausage, Ro*tel, and cream cheese are blended together well.

Serve with tortilla chips and enjoy!

◆◆◆◆◆◆◆◆◆◆◆◆◆◆◆◆◆◆◆◆◆◆◆◆◆◆◆◆◆◆◆◆◆◆◆◆◆◆◆◆◆◆◆◆

# THRASH KEBABS

## Jeff Paulick, *Lazarus A.D.*

**D**uring the entire process of cooking be sure to indulge in several marijuana joints and several Miller Lites. In fact, before you start anything, be sure to have one of each.

**SERVES 4 TO 6 DRUNK GUYS**

24-pack Miller Lite (2 beers for the recipe, 22 for you and your friends to drink)
½ cup A.1. Chicago Steakhouse Marinade
¼ cup Jimi Mac's Super Sauce hot sauce
1 teaspoon onion powder
1 teaspoon garlic powder
½ teaspoon red pepper flakes
1½ pounds beef chuck tender steak
1 red onion

¼ pound serrano chiles
1 green bell pepper
1 red bell pepper
1 yellow bell pepper
½ cup olive oil
1 cup pineapple cubes
½ teaspoon salt
½ teaspoon ground black pepper

First prepare the marinade in a large bowl. Pour 2 beers into a bowl, add the marinade, hot sauce, onion powder, garlic powder, and red pepper flakes, then mix together.

Cut the steak into 1- to 2-inch cubes and place in the marinade. Cover with aluminum foil, place in the refrigerator, and allow to marinate for 12 to 24 hours.

Cut onion into eight wedges. Cut the serrano chiles into ½-inch sections. Cut the green, red, and yellow bell peppers into 1- to 2-inch squares (use of the separate colored bell peppers will make the kebabs more vibrant and therefore more delicious).

Brush 6 metal skewers with some olive oil. Alternate bell peppers, onion pieces, pineapple cubes, serrano chiles, and drained steak cubes on the skewers. Brush

more olive oil over the kebabs so they don't burn. Sprinkle salt and black pepper over the kebabs.

Using a paper towel, spread a layer of olive oil on grill grate so the kebabs don't stick to grate. Preheat the grill (charcoal or gas) to about 300°F. Place the kebabs on the grill and cook for 7 to 8 minutes, then rotate and cook for another 7 to 8 minutes (keep on longer for a more well-done kebab). Enjoy!

# STUFFED POBLANO PEPPERS
# WITH CHIPS AND SALSA

### Trevor Peres, *Obituary*

This is probably one of my favorite Mexican-style recipes. It's kind of a spin-off of chiles rellenos. The poblano pepper gives off some spicy heat compared to the green bell pepper, which is generally used in a chile relleno. Also, you don't get a "stuffed" feeling after you eat the stuffed poblano peppers as you can with chiles rellenos. I think it's because there is a lot less cheese in my recipe. The funny thing is, I still get "stuffed" after eating the stuffed poblano peppers as much as eating chiles rellenos. Probably because I eat more than one person should eat of the stuffed poblano peppers. That is the good thing about this recipe. It is so good you can't stop eating it. I hope you enjoy my stuffed poblano peppers. Happy eating!!!

SERVES 3

3 poblano peppers
Olive oil
1 pound ground beef
Salt
1 small yellow onion, finely chopped
1 garlic clove, finely chopped
¾ teaspoon chili powder
½ teaspoon ground cumin
¼ teaspoon onion powder
¼ teaspoon garlic powder
¼ teaspoon cayenne pepper
¼ cup water
¼ pound shredded cheddar cheese
 (about 1 cup)
Salsa and chips, for serving (recipe follows)
Refried beans, heated, for serving

Rub the poblano peppers with olive oil and place under broiler until skin starts to turn a little brown. Rotate a few times to brown evenly. Take out of the oven and put the peppers in a plastic bowl and cover tightly for 30 minutes so pepper can sweat. Peel the skin off the peppers, cut a slit in the side of each pepper, and remove the seeds. Set aside.

◆◆◆◆◆◆◆◆◆◆◆◆◆◆◆◆◆◆◆◆◆◆◆◆◆◆◆◆◆◆◆◆◆◆◆◆◆◆◆◆◆◆◆◆◆◆◆

Brown the ground beef in a skillet with ½ teaspoon salt. When brown, drain off the fat and set the meat aside. Add the onion, garlic, and 2 tablespoons olive oil to the skillet and sauté. Add the browned beef, chili powder, cumin, onion powder, garlic powder, cayenne, water, and a pinch of salt. Heat while stirring frequently until water cooks out.

Fill each poblano pepper with one-third of the beef mixture and cover with shredded cheddar. Place under the broiler until cheese melts, 3 to 4 minutes. Pour a little salsa on top of each pepper and serve with some warm refried beans on the side with chips and salsa.

## SALSA AND CHIPS

½ small yellow onion

3 garlic cloves

Fresh cilantro

One 14.5-ounce can petite diced tomatoes, drained

Juice of 1 lime

Salt

1 bag your favorite tortilla chips

Finely mince the onion and garlic, chop up 2 tablespoons worth of cilantro, and combine with the tomatoes. Stir in the lime juice and salt to taste. Chill for 1 hour before serving with tortilla chips.

# METAL MUSHROOM TUNA MELT

## John Alaia, *Moth Eater*

⊕ ur first time making this meal, I was cooking the caps in the broiler (which is on the bottom of my old-school oven) and I noticed a smell which I thought at the time was the broiler burning the olive oil on the caps. Eh, whatever. I just kept on trucking with the cooking. Well, as the cheese was melting on the caps, I had realized that I hadn't emptied the oven of all its storage contents. I had left a pink plastic baking tray (my wife's cupcake thingy) in the regular part of the oven along with some baking sheets and pans and the plastic thing had melted and dripped down into the broiler and all over everything. I opened my oven and white noxious smoke filled my entire apartment. I flung all windows and doors open, and all the plastic covered materials were then tossed outside onto the lawn (leaving burn marks in the grass). The wife and I quickly threw our cats in the bedroom and fanned as much smoke out the doors as we could. Nevertheless, we ate the Tuna Melts anyway and probably ingested tons of toxic plastic. Delicious! Cook Safe!

SERVES 2

4 large portobello mushroom caps, stemmed, with the gills removed

3 tablespoons olive oil

One 6-ounce can albacore tuna in water, drained

½ cup chopped parsley

1 celery stalk, diced if preferred (I hate that shit)

2 tablespoons lemon juice

½ teaspoon salt

¼ teaspoon ground pepper

½ teaspoon garlic powder

¼ teaspoon onion powder

4 slices your favorite cheese (I prefer white American)

Preheat your broiler. While your broiler is preheating, brush your mushroom caps with 2 tablespoons of the oil. Paint that shit on like Picasso. Throw the oiled caps on a baking sheet, rimmed for her pleasure >:). Broil them for about 10 minutes, flipping them one time halfway through. They should be soft and cooked through. They may shrink like your dick after stepping out of the pool, but that's normal.

While the 'shrooms are cooking, throw your tuna (mash it with a fork), parsley, celery (if you like that nasty shit), lemon juice, salt, pepper, garlic powder, onion powder, and your remaining oil in a big mixing bowl (so you don't spill). Mix them up real nice.

Once your 'shrooms are done cooking, divide the tuna mixture amongst the four caps. Make sure you spread the mixture as evenly as possible or you're gonna spill that shit all over your new Moth Eater T-shirt when you take a bite. Top each one with a slice of your favorite artery-clogging, heart-stopping cheese. Throw them back in the broiler until the cheese melts, which is roughly 2 minutes.

Crack open your coldest can of Natty Ice and enjoy your new favorite dinner!

♦♦♦♦♦♦♦♦♦♦♦♦♦♦♦♦♦♦♦♦♦♦♦♦♦♦♦♦♦♦♦♦♦♦♦♦♦♦♦♦♦♦♦♦♦♦♦

# CHEESE 'N' EGG PARTY PUFFS

## Andrew W.K.

**MAKES ABOUT 48 PARTY PUFFS DEPENDING ON THE SIZE
OF THE MOUNDS AND HOW HARD YOU PARTY**

2 cups of water
8 tablespoons (1 stick) butter, cut into chunks
1½ cups all-purpose flour
6 large eggs, beaten
1¼ cups shredded sharp white cheddar cheese
1½ teaspoons freshly ground pepper
Coarse sea salt

Preheat the oven to 400°F.

In a 4-quart saucepan over high heat, bring the water and butter to a full, rolling boil. Remove from heat and add the flour all at once, stirring until mixture is a smooth, thick paste with no lumps. Add a quarter of the beaten eggs at a time, stirring vigorously after each addition. Stir in the cheese and pepper.

Spoon the dough into a plastic zipper bag. Cut off one small corner of the bag, and pipe small mounds onto buttered baking sheets. Sprinkle each mound with the sea salt.

Bake for about 30 minutes, until golden brown. Serve warm.

◆◆◆◆◆◆◆◆◆◆◆◆◆◆◆◆◆◆◆◆◆◆◆◆◆◆◆◆◆◆◆◆◆◆◆◆◆◆◆◆◆◆◆◆◆◆◆◆

# NACHOS

## Mark Hunter, *Chimaira*

SERVES 4

1 green bell pepper
1 red bell pepper
1 orange bell pepper
Half 12-ounce jar banana peppers, drained
Half 12-ounce jar pitted green olives
Salt and pepper
Frank's Red Hot Sauce
Cayenne pepper
1 pint baby tomatoes or cherry
  tomatoes (use about half)

2 pounds ground beef
One 1.25-ounce packet Taco Bell
  Taco Seasoning
4 tablespoons (½ stick) unsalted
  butter
One 24-ounce bag Tostitos tortilla
  chips
One 15.5-ounce jar Taco Bell Salsa
  con Queso (medium)
Sour cream

Chop the green, red, and orange peppers, banana peppers, and olives and put them all together in a large bowl. Add salt, pepper, Frank's Red Hot Sauce, and cayenne pepper to taste (desired amount for spicy tastes), and mix them all together. Let marinate for about an hour.

Put the tomatoes in a separate bowl and salt them.

In a large skillet, cook the ground beef until browned, breaking it up with a spoon as it cooks. Drain off the fat. Add the taco seasoning and salt, pepper, cayenne, and Frank's Red Hot Sauce to taste (desired amount for spicy tastes).

In another large skillet over medium-high heat, melt the butter. When butter is almost melted, add the vegetables and cook until tender. Turn the burner to low and add the tomatoes. Keep on low heat until ready to put the nachos together.

Get out a big plate and pile on the tortilla chips, top with the meat, then the vegetables. Microwave the Salsa con Queso and pour over. Top with sour cream. Eat and enjoy!

# FRESH TUNA NIÇOISE SALAD

## Scott Rockenfield, *Queensrÿche*

**T**his recipe holds a special place for me for a few reasons. Mainly, it was the first dinner I cooked for my wife when we first met back in 1994. I had always liked seared tuna, and this seemed like an excellent presentation to have a romantic dinner together. So far, so good. We have been married now for thirteen years and have three beautiful kids!

SERVES 2

½ pound fresh yellowfin tuna
5 tiny red potatoes, halved
15 to 20 thin green beans, trimmed
1 small tomato
½ small red bell pepper
½ small green bell pepper
¼ small red onion
1 head red leaf lettuce
6 to 8 ounces kalamata olives
½ cup vinaigrette dressing, made with equal parts extra virgin olive oil
    and balsamic vinegar and flavored with fresh basil and garlic
Salt and pepper

Preheat a cast iron ridged grill pan. Add the tuna steak and "flash grill," searing it for roughly 1 to 2 minutes per side so that the middle retains its beautiful pink color. Allow to cool, then cut into large chunks.

In a medium pot of boiling water, cook the potatoes until fork-tender, about 20 minutes. Remove with a slotted spoon and set aside to cool, then chill.

Bring the water back to a boil. Add the beans and cook for 1 to 2 minutes to blanch. Drain, rinse under cold water, and chill.

◆◆◆◆◆◆◆◆◆◆◆◆◆◆◆◆◆◆◆◆◆◆◆◆◆◆◆◆◆◆◆◆◆◆◆◆◆◆◆◆◆◆◆◆◆◆◆◆◆

Cut the tomato, red and green peppers, and the onion into large chunks.

Arrange the seared tuna somewhat centered on the serving dish on top of a bed of red lettuce.

Then in a circular fashion place the remaining items around the tuna. Once arranged, sprinkle with the vinaigrette, salt and pepper to taste.

Now—Enjoy!!!

# REMO'S HOT, SWEET, AND STICKY ASS-KICKIN' CHICKEN WINGS

### Jeremy Thompson, *Nashville Pussy*

⊕ h shit y'all! These wings are awesome!! Basically I've taken about five different wing recipes and Frankensteined them together over time with a few of my own twists. I made four dozen of these for a 4th of July party, and they were gone lickity split. No shit. I'm a big fan of wings. They are cheap and pretty easy to make. PLUS you can eat them with your hands like Conan!!!! What is best in life? To crush your enemies, to see them driven before you, and to hear the lamentations of their women. AND to eat badass chicken wings!! You will super like these wings!!!! I promise. They are good. I know what's up!! Enjoy.

SERVES 4 TO 6

2 pounds chicken wings, tips removed, cut in half at the joint
¾ cup ketchup
¼ cup balsamic vinegar
1 tablespoon dark brown sugar
1½ ounces (1 shot) Dr Pepper
4 teaspoons garlic powder
4 teaspoons Worcestershire sauce
4 teaspoons Tabasco sauce
2 teaspoons Dijon mustard
2 teaspoons paprika
2 teaspoons chili powder
2 teaspoons cayenne pepper

Rinse wings with water and pat dry. Mix together all the other ingredients in a large plastic zipper bag and add the wings. Press the air out of the bag and close. Work the sauce around the chicken. Place the bag in a bowl and refrigerate for 2 to 6 hours.

Light a charcoal grill when you're ready to cook. Separate the coals so they're in two piles, one on each side of the grate.

Place the wings directly over the coals and grill for about 5 minutes, turning once. Then move to the center of the grill so they're not directly over the coals. Cook for another 10 minutes, or until meat isn't pink at the bone.

Enjoy your wings with some grilled corn and ice cold beer. BAGAWK!!

# HEADLINERS

# THE BEST DAMN MAC AND CHEESE IN THE WHOLE DAMN UNIVERSE

### Steve "Buckshot" Seabury, *Moth Eater*

This has to be one of my personal favorite recipes. I love it so much that I want to share it with you. I remember my mom always making this when I was a kid. When she would cook it up the whole house would smell so yummy that my sisters and I would drool with anticipation of all the cheesy gooey madness. If we didn't do our chores, I knew deep down inside that we wouldn't get this childhood, tasty treat.

My wife and I have changed it a little, but we still make it a lot. I can't wait to share this recipe with my kids and I hope they share it with theirs.

Before you even get started, turn up the stereo and crack open a can of your favorite beer. Yes, I said can of beer. I would recommend "Kings of Metal" by Manowar.

Enjoy.

SERVES 4

16 ounces elbow macaroni (I like to use whole-wheat pasta now)
One 7-ounce brick white Heluva Good! Extra Sharp cheddar cheese
One 7-ounce brick white Heluva Good! Sharp cheddar cheese
3 ounces Swiss cheese
2 ounces smoked gouda cheese
1½ cups milk
5 tablespoons all-purpose flour
Freshly ground black pepper

Bring water to a boil and dump in the elbow macaroni. I like to throw some salt in the water to give the macaroni some added flavor. Let them cook until those suckers are done. Drain.

◆◆◆◆◆◆◆◆◆◆◆◆◆◆◆◆◆◆◆◆◆◆◆◆◆◆◆◆◆◆◆◆◆◆◆◆◆◆◆◆◆◆◆◆◆◆◆◆◆

Take the blocks of cheese and grate them into a large bowl. Once they are all grated, stir them all together.

Take a separate bowl and pour the milk and flour into it. Take a whisk and whip it up so there are no clumps of flour floating around.

Take your medium casserole. Take a couple of scoops of macaroni and place them in the bowl. Throw a handful of the cheese on top. Repeat layer after layer until you reach the top of the dish. I like to add a dash of freshly ground pepper in between each layer.

Once you get all the layers built, take your milk-flour mixture and dump it in. Let them noodles enjoy the swim.

Preheat your oven to 350°F. Once the oven is warmed up, place your casserole into the center of the oven. Cook for 25 minutes or until done. You will know it's done when you see the cheese on the top layer get all nice and crusty. This is my wife's favorite part of the meal. I do have to agree with her.

Let it sit for 5 minutes to settle and cool down. Crack open another can of beer and enjoy.

◆◆◆◆◆◆◆◆◆◆◆◆◆◆◆◆◆◆◆◆◆◆◆◆◆◆◆◆◆◆◆◆◆◆◆◆◆◆◆◆◆◆◆◆◆

# MARK'S SUPER AWESOME MARINARA

## Mark Morton, *Lamb of God*

This is my favorite recipe because I love Italian food. It's *really* easy, and it's better than any of that store-bought garbage. Hope you enjoy!

**SERVES 4**

**1 big pour olive oil** (I like the extra virgin type best, because it tastes rowdier)

**1 big handful chopped fresh garlic** (do *not* substitute with dried or powdered . . . it'll suck)

**14.5 ounces stewed tomatoes** (your favorite brand)

**1 small handful salt** (you may need more, but we'll get to that)

**1 big handful sugar**

**A couple pinches black pepper and/or red pepper flakes**

**A couple pinches of something green and Italian-ish** . . . whatever you have . . .
   fresh basil leaves are great, but dried oregano or generic "Italian Seasoning" . . .
   whatever's lying around

Pour the olive oil into a medium saucepan. Add the garlic and simmer over low heat until the garlic starts to look kind of translucent.

Add the tomatoes, and let them simmer for a couple minutes. Use a wooden spoon to mix them with the garlic and oil. You can turn up the heat a little bit, but not too high . . . this is a slow cookin' kind of deal.

Add the salt, sugar, pepper, green stuff, and whatnot . . . use your taste buds to determine how much. Don't be shy with the sugar—it should be as sweet as it is salty. That's kind of the secret to it.

Simmer over low heat for an hour or so, stirring occasionally, to let the sauce thicken up. Taste it every once in a while to see if it needs more salt or sugar or pepper. Don't burn your tongue! I *always* do.

# STAGE STEW

## Tracii Guns, *LA Guns*

I started ordering this from Bob's Big Boy when I was about six years old. It is very tasty and very filling. Later, when I was launching my music career, I would always ask my mother to make it for me for dinner. Now when I am on tour in the States, Skyline Chili makes a compact frozen version that fits perfectly in a tour bus freezer (twenty containers), so more times than not, that is what I eat about two hours before I go on stage.

Boil the pasta. Cook the Dennison's Chili con Carne with Beans. Put the pasta on a plate. Put 1 slice American cheese on top of the pasta. Cover with chili, and sprinkle a bunch of shredded cheddar cheese on top, along with a dollop of sour cream. Wash down with ice-cold Coca-Cola.

◆◆◆◆◆◆◆◆◆◆◆◆◆◆◆◆◆◆◆◆◆◆◆◆◆◆◆◆◆◆◆◆◆◆◆◆◆◆◆◆◆◆◆◆◆◆

# JÄGERMEISTER ROASTED LAMB

## Brandon Eedy, *Baptized In Blood*

I t's a little fancy, and we like to believe we can actually cook. Gives you energy and protein, and the remaining booze you don't use gets you drunk. Plus, it's a good combination of two things we love: *meat* and *Jägermeister*.

**SERVES 2**

¼ cup extra virgin olive oil

¼ cup fresh rosemary leaves,
   or about 1 tablespoon dry

10 garlic cloves

1 bottle Jägermeister (¼ cup to cook,
   the rest to pound)

Salt

Freshly ground black pepper

1 or 2 frenched racks of lamb (about
   1 pound total)

¾ cup cabernet sauvignon

2 teaspoons cornstarch

1 cup cold water

1 tablespoon butter

Preheat the oven to 375°F.

Blend the olive oil, rosemary, garlic, ¼ cup of the Jägermeister, 1 teaspoon salt, and 2 teaspoons pepper in a food processor or blender.

Cover the tips of the lamb bones with aluminum foil. Rub the rosemary mixture over the lamb and place bone side down in a roasting pan. Roast 25 minutes for rare, 30 minutes for medium-rare, or 35 minutes for medium. Remove from oven and tent with foil.

Place the roasting pan over medium-high heat on your stovetop and pour in the wine. Scrape the caramelized bits (fond) off the bottom of the pan with a wooden spoon.

Dissolve the cornstarch in the water and whisk into roasting pan along with the butter. Strain the gravy through a fine-mesh strainer and season with salt and pepper to taste.

To serve, cut between bones and teepee over brown rice, couscous, or the like.

◆◆◆◆◆◆◆◆◆◆◆◆◆◆◆◆◆◆◆◆◆◆◆◆◆◆◆◆◆◆◆◆◆◆◆◆◆◆◆◆◆◆◆◆◆◆◆◆◆◆

# SATANIC BURRITO

### Joel Grind, *Toxic Holocaust*

First off, I know everyone is wondering why I've submitted a vegan recipe. My mind is even kinda blown, but the real reason is that this is honestly delicious. This dish was first made for me by the PDX metal queen Jozy Pants. I was fully meat eating at the time and she was vegan, but she made me this and it kinda opened my eyes to the fact that not all vegetarian food tastes like cardboard. Try it out!

**SERVES 4 OR 5**

2 medium baking potatoes, cubed
3 tablespoons vegetable oil
1 small onion, diced
1 red or green bell pepper, diced
1½ tablespoons red curry paste
1 large tomato, diced

1½ tablespoons brown sugar
One 20-ounce package super firm tofu, cubed
One 11.5-ounce package large flour tortillas
Veganaise
Tapatio or other hot sauce

Microwave the potatoes in a covered bowl for 3 minutes. Heat oil in large skillet over medium heat. Add the potatoes to the oil and cook until lightly brown. Add onions. Once the onions start to brown, add the peppers and curry paste (more or less to taste), and stir until all veggies are tender. Add the tomatoes and cook for 2 minutes more. Once all veggies are cooked, remove from the pan and set aside in a large bowl.

In the same large pan you used to cook veggies, heat the brown sugar over medium heat. When it starts to bubble, add the tofu and stir until the tofu is coated. Cook the tofu until it is golden and firm. Add the cooked veggies back into the pan. Reduce the heat to low.

In a separate pan over high heat, warm the tortillas. Spread a thin layer of Veganaise on each tortilla and fill with veg-tofu mixture. Add hot sauce and stuff your beak.

✦✦✦✦✦✦✦✦✦✦✦✦✦✦✦✦✦✦✦✦✦✦✦✦✦✦✦✦✦✦✦✦✦✦✦✦✦✦✦✦✦✦✦

# CALIFORNIA EGGS BENEDICT

## Dizzy Reed, *Guns N' Roses*

California-style eggs benedict is a bit of a healthier twist on the beat-up and abused room service version that we eat all the time. It calls for turkey instead of Canadian bacon or ham, so if you ain't down with the pork, it's a good alternative. And it's one more use for that leftover bird during the holidaze. Avocado gives it another California fresh flavor that puts it over the top. It's awesome for Sunday brunch before the big game, perfect for hangovers, and a great way to impress your chick the next morning. If done properly, it can almost make you feel like you're as cool as that Naked Chef guy. Just don't cook it naked. That could leave a different impression altogether.

SERVES 2

4 eggs

2 English muffins, halved

1 packet hollandaise sauce mix

4 slices leftover fresh roasted turkey or thick-sliced deli turkey

½ ripe avocado, pitted, peeled, and sliced

Pinch of paprika

Pinch of ground black pepper

Pinch of chopped fresh parsley

Poach the eggs in an egg poacher or the really hard ol' fashioned way in simmering water. Cook them to your liking but don't over cook them!! As anyone who appreciates eggs benedict knows, they need to be at least a little bit runny.

While the eggs are cooking, toast the muffin halves and whip together the hollandaise sauce so it's nice and fresh and hot.

In the meantime, put a small skillet on low heat. Arrange two plates with two muffin halves each, throw the turkey slices in the skillet for just about 30 seconds, turning them once, to heat them up with a little bit of the flavor (posers may throw it in the microwave).

Layer each muffin half with turkey, then avocado, then an egg, and top with hollandaise. Sprinkle a little bit of paprika, pepper, and parsley on top and serve with some freshly squeezed O.J. or a Bloody Mary. Enjoy!

# BAKED MACARONI AND CHEESE BALLS

## Michael Starr, *Steel Panther*

I love to make this dish on my birthday, and I'll tell you why. I remember when I was just getting my feet wet in Hollywood. The band and I would hang out at a strip club called Crazy Girls. Because we had nowhere to live, we would hang out there all day and all night. I would hit on a stripper that was working the late shift and convince her to let me hook up with her and that way I would have a place to sleep for the night. It worked out so good for all of us. This one stripper, her name was Brandy. Well, her real name was Britney Cashtonolph. I think she was Italian. She took me in one night and really pounded the shit out of me. I mean she was on top the whole time, I was watching MTV while she was going to town. It was my birthday, and I told her, so she said, "I'll make you dinner." I went to the bathroom to wipe her stuff off of me and I realized I really needed a shower. I had a bad case of "ball cheese." You know, when your balls smell like cheese. I took a shower and came out for dinner. She said, "I made my dad's favorite dish, Classic Baked Macaroni and Cheese Balls." I just about lost it right in front of her. But I have to admit it was tasty, and I make it every year now for anyone who is with me on my birthday. So enjoy this. It's really good with Top Ramen.

SERVES 6

Nonstick cooking spray
1 tablespoon unsalted butter or nonhydrogenated margarine
2 tablespoons all-purpose flour
2 tablespoons garlic powder
1 tablespoon onion powder
2 cups skim milk
½ cup shredded reduced-fat sharp cheddar cheese
2 tablespoons grated Parmesan cheese
Salt and pepper (optional)

½ pound (2 cups) conchiglie (shell-shape) pasta, cooked according to package
    directions and drained
½ cup panko bread crumbs

Preheat the oven to 350°F. Coat a 6-cup baking dish with cooking spray.

Melt the butter in a saucepan over medium heat. Add the flour, garlic powder, and onion powder, and cook 1 minute, whisking constantly. Slowly whisk in the milk. Increase the heat to medium-high and bring the sauce to a boil, whisking constantly. Reduce the heat to medium-low and simmer 5 minutes, stirring occasionally.

Remove from the heat and stir in the cheddar and Parmesan. Season with salt and pepper, if desired. Stir in the cooked pasta. Transfer to the baking dish and top with the bread crumbs. Lightly spray the bread crumbs with cooking spray. Bake 30 minutes, or until top begins to brown.

# IRON QUICHE

## Adam Wakeman, *Ozzy Osbourne*

I'm not going to jump on the "gravy train" with this one. I'm presenting a genuine Wakeman recipe that I cook at least thirteen times every week.

It's healthy, so no need to be "frying high again," and for me, as a vegetarian, poultry dishes such as "Mr. Fowley" are right out. If you are feeling adventurous, feel free to knock up a "No More Tiramisu" as a perfect dessert.

Simply pour yourself a beer or a "Sherry Mason" and get cooking.

**SERVES 4**

Enough pie crust pastry to line an 8-inch quiche pan
½ pound green asparagus, woody bottoms snapped off
⅔ cup heavy cream
2 large eggs
1 handful fresh parsley, chopped
Salt and pepper
1 teaspoon Dijon mustard
3½ ounces cheddar cheese, grated (about 1 cup)
3½ ounces Red Leicester or similar cheese, grated (about 1 cup)

Preheat the oven to 375°F. Roll out the pastry and line an 8-inch quiche pan. Prick in several places with a fork. Bake for 15 minutes. Remove from the oven (but leave the oven on).

Wash the asparagus thoroughly to remove any grit and chop into 2-inch chunks. Steam lightly for 5 minutes, then drain well.

Beat together the cream and eggs. Add the parsley, salt and pepper to taste, and the mustard. Put half of each cheese into the cream mixture.

Arrange the asparagus spears in the quiche pan (obviously in the shape of a crucifix . . .) and pour the cream mixture on top. Sprinkle the remaining cheese on top.

Bake for about 35 minutes (this depends on your oven), until the egg mixture has risen and set.

◆◆◆◆◆◆◆◆◆◆◆◆◆◆◆◆◆◆◆◆◆◆◆◆◆◆◆◆◆◆◆◆◆◆◆◆◆◆◆◆◆◆◆◆◆◆◆◆

# KALE 'EM ALL

## Liam Wilson, *Dillinger Escape Plan*

I love this dish because it's cheap, really easy to make quickly, and is made up almost entirely of green leafy vegetables, which aren't hard to find or prepare.

**SERVES 3 OR 4**

2 tablespoons extra virgin olive oil

1 teaspoon ground black pepper

1 bunch kale (about 2½ pounds), washed, stemmed, and shredded
   into bite-size portions

¼ cup water

½ cup chopped fresh dill

½ cup chopped fresh parsley

Sea salt

Juice of 1 lime

Pinch of cayenne pepper (optional)

Cue up Metallica's oft-overlooked classic *Kill 'em All* and press play. Heat the oil in a large skillet with black pepper, tell the kale leaves to "Jump In The Fire," and sauté for 3 to 4 minutes, or until "Hit The Lights" is ending. Add the water, cover, and allow to steam for 3 to 4 minutes or until kale is tender and "The Four Horsemen" breakdown is reminding you that Famine is something you ironically will not have to endure for too much longer, and Death will hopefully be prolonged because of your healthy dietary choice to eat this dish, which requires little to "No Remorse." Remove from the heat and mix in dill, parsley, sea salt to taste, lime juice, and cayenne (if using). "Seek . . ." out a place "and Destroy" this meal immediately.

◆◆◆◆◆◆◆◆◆◆◆◆◆◆◆◆◆◆◆◆◆◆◆◆◆◆◆◆◆◆◆◆◆◆◆◆◆◆◆◆◆◆◆◆◆◆◆◆

# FAST GARLIC CHICKEN OD

## Kenny Winter, *Exciter*

This is something I made a few years ago. I had invited a girl over for a dinner date, and I was running late. I originally wanted to make something special, but time was short. So I ran down to the supermarket, stupid me forgetting my credit card and with only $14 in my pocket, but I had plenty of time, ninety minutes. I whipped this up in thirty minutes, having it ready to serve as the doorbell rang. BTW, she wasn't early. Like an idiot I also locked myself out of the apartment, and it took me forty minutes to find my super and get back in. But I got laid! Yes . . . despite the garlic.

SERVES 4

1 Exciter CD intact

1 CD player

2 pounds skinless, boneless chicken breast

One 15-ounce bottle lemon juice

Seasoning salt (do not season the CDs)

1 tablespoon crumbled sage

1 cup fresh sliced garlic

2 tablespoons butter or margarine

2 tablespoons canola or vegetable oil

1 medium onion, chopped

½ cup garlic paste

One 18.8-ounce can of Campbell's Select Harvest Creamy Potato
   with Roasted Garlic Soup

Now the beauty of this recipe is that you don't have to follow it to the letter. It's primarily done to taste.

This whole process should take about 30 minutes. Make sure an Exciter album is playing in the background. It adds to the flavor.

First take the chicken breasts and rinse thoroughly using the lemon juice and water to clean them. Cut them into 1-inch cubes. Season to taste with seasoning salt and sage.

Set large skillet over medium heat and roast the sliced garlic in the pan with 1 tablespoon of the butter until it turns a light gold. Add the chicken, the rest of the butter and the oil. Heat until you're satisfied it's just shy of fully cooked, then add the onion and the garlic paste while stirring it to full mix. Raise the heat to about medium-high and add the soup, enough to coat the chicken. I personally add about three quarters of the can to cover 2 pounds of chicken. Stir and cook until the soup is fully heated.

# THE HEAVY STEW

## Ash Pearson, *3 Inches of Blood*

I was introduced to hearty meals by my parents at an early age. Leftover chilis and soups were always great for staying warm in a very cold Saskatoon winter in Canada. This stew includes all my favorite vegetable and spice ingredients, plus a generous portion of meat. A friend of mine named Curtis Dean introduced me to the idea of adding Coca-Cola to stew and to dumplings. Truly satisfying!

FEEDS THE WHOLE BAND

**FOR THE STEW**

Olive oil

1 pound cubed stew beef

All-purpose flour

4 to 6 Yukon gold potatoes, cut into bite-size chunks

1 to 5 garlic cloves, minced

2 medium onions, chopped

2 celery stalks, chopped

2 or 3 large carrots, chopped

1 or 2 bell peppers (color of your choice), chopped

Fresh corn kernels, peas, diced beets, or cut green beans (your choice, optional)

Italian seasoning

Paprika

1 bay leaf

2 tablespoons white wine vinegar

2 glugs balsamic vinegar

Hot sauce

A few pours of Worcestershire sauce

2½ cups chicken stock

One 12-ounce Coke

1 cup spiral pasta

**FOR THE DUMPLINGS**

⅔ cup all-purpose flour

1 teaspoon baking powder

⅛ teaspoon salt

2 teaspoons dried herbs (your choice) or Italian seasoning

¼ cup milk

2 tablespoons vegetable oil

◆◆◆◆◆◆◆◆◆◆◆◆◆◆◆◆◆◆◆◆◆◆◆◆◆◆◆◆◆◆◆◆◆◆◆◆◆◆◆◆◆◆◆◆◆◆◆◆◆◆◆◆◆

Heat a few pours of olive oil in a large soup pot. Coat the beef in flour and add to oil. Fry for 3 to 5 minutes until brown. Add the potatoes, garlic, and onions. Fry until the onions are transparent, about 5 minutes. Turn the heat down to medium-low. Add the celery, carrots, peppers, and any other extra vegetables you wish and cook for about 5 minutes.

Time to get some liquid in there. Add Italian seasoning, paprika, the bay leaf, vinegars, hot sauce, Worcestershire sauce, chicken stock, and Coke. The Coke tenderizes the meat and goes really well with the other savory flavors. Check the liquid level. Add the pasta. The ingredients should be well-pooled in liquid. Turn the heat up to high, bring to a boil then turn down to a low simmer. Cover and simmer for about an hour.

With about 20 minutes left, it's time to make the dumplings. Combine the flour, baking powder, salt, and dried herbs. Mix the milk and oil, then add to dry ingredients. Mix until just combined. Do not overmix.

Drop dumplings by large tablespoonfuls on top of the stew; do not stir in the dumplings or flip them over. Cover and do not lift lid. Just let them sit on top of the stew and cook from the heat. They will turn into a chewy, bread texture, which goes great with the stew. Cook for about 20 minutes, lift lid and poke dumplings with a toothpick. If the toothpick comes out dry, they are done.

Enjoy!

# BBQ GRILL PIZZA

## Keri Kelli, *Alice Cooper*

**G**rilled pizzas are a specific style of pie: thin-crusted, with minimal toppings. Cheeses won't turn brown, since there's no upper heat source. These pizzas are lightly sauced, since too much liquid can cause the crust to become soggy and difficult to transfer from the grill. They're also very fast baking. Although the high heat of the grill produces a truly excellent pizza, it's a challenge to get a perfectly cooked crisp crust at the same time the toppings are ready. But after years of trial and error (and much help from my Italian comrade, Phil Costantini), I've developed a fairly foolproof way to get perfect pizzas every time. With grilled pizza, the crust is the star—think of it as a great flatbread.

Another great partner in the quest for the ultimate BBQ Grill Pizza is my buddy Tom Seefurth at Mamma Mia! They supply me with all the dough mix, spice, and Pizza Beer (yes, that's right Pizza Beer!) to perfectly complement this recipe. Go to www.mammamiapizzabeer.com for more info.

Of course you can use a store-bought dough for these grilled pizzas (Trader Joe's and Whole Foods have great premade dough), but making one yourself doesn't involve much work; the kneading is almost meditative. With all of the fresh ingredients, these pizzas are off the chain!

SERVES 4, WITH LEFTOVERS FOR BREAKFAST

1 package Mamma Mia! Pizza Beer Crust Mix

1 tablespoon extra virgin olive oil or melted butter

One 12-ounce bottle Mamma Mia! Pizza Beer or your favorite microbrew

All-purpose flour

One 15-ounce can Eden Organic Pizza-Pasta Sauce (or any available authentic pizza sauce you can find)

1 package Mamma Mia! Pizza Sauce Spice Mix

Cornmeal

One 8-ounce ball fresh buffalo mozzarella, grated

Marguerita toppings: 2 minced garlic cloves, 6 chopped Roma (plum) tomatoes, chopped fresh basil leaves (from 1 bunch)

Vegetarian toppings: one 15-ounce can quartered artichokes (I use Maria brand), 1 chopped medium red onion, 6-chopped Roma (plum) tomatoes, 2 chopped bell peppers (mix up the colors—we usually use red, yellow, or orange)

¼ cup freshly grated Parmesan (optional)

Red pepper flakes (optional)

## Prepping the grill

Fire up the grill with your pizza stones on the grill. Your pizzas will cook best on a hot (600°F+) grill, so make sure to allow time for it to heat up. A gas grill should be turned to high to begin with. Once the grill has reached 600°F, turn all burners to low.

## Making the dough

Empty the contents of your crust mix into a large bowl and create a well in the middle. Combine the olive oil and beer, and mix thoroughly by hand—it will be a bit loose and sticky.

Turn the dough out onto a lightly floured surface and fold it over itself a few times, kneading until it's smooth and elastic. Get a feel for the dough by squeezing a small amount together. If it's crumbly, add more beer! If it's sticky, add a bit of flour. Knead until the dough gathers into a ball. This should take about 5 minutes. Form the dough into a round ball and split into two equal halves.

Cover and let rest for 15 minutes, so it will be easier to roll out. In the meantime, prep the pizza toppings.

## Making the sauce

Empty the can of sauce into a large bowl and combine with the spice mix. Mix thoroughly with a wooden spoon.

## Making the pies

To roll out the dough balls, lightly flour a work surface. Shape or roll each ball into a rustic oblong shape, about ¼ inch thick and 10 to 12 inches long.

Sprinkle cornmeal on your pizza peel (that's a big pizza spatula!) and carefully slide your dough onto it. Evenly spread your desired amount of sauce onto the crust and top with mozzarella. Top with the Marguerita toppings or the vegetarian toppings. (Or use any toppings you like—that's why making your own pizza at home is so killer!)

## Grilling

Once you have the pizzas ready on the pizza peels, lightly move the pizza peel to check that the pizza crust is not stuck anywhere.

Open the grill, sprinkle a little cornmeal on the pizza stones to ensure nothing sticks. Slide the pies onto the pizza stones. Once they are in place, cover the grill and cook for 5 to 7 minutes.

You can check on the pizza every few minutes, but try not to open the cover too often, otherwise the pizzas will not cook thoroughly. Continue to grill until the toppings are cooked to your liking.

Be sure to check the bottom of the dough. The only tricky part to grilling pizza is to not let the crust burn. Cook until the bottom is nicely browned and crisp.

Remove the pizza from grill and admire your work! Then cut and serve. Don't forget to add any additional items, such as freshly grated Parmesan or red pepper flakes.

# RICK'S PRISON "SPREAD"

## Dexter Holland, *The Offspring*

I have this friend, Rick. A while back I was looking for recipes to go with my hot sauce, Gringo Bandito, and he shared this one with me. You see, Rick has spent some time behind bars. So I'm inclined to believe him when he tells me what someone is willing to do in prison for a good meal. Plus it's got a great kick. Enjoy!

Top Ramen (1 package per person)
1 trash bag
Other crap
Gringo Bandito Hot Sauce (or whatever hot sauce floats yer boat,
    but Gringo Bandito really is the best!)
Crunchy Cheetos

The main ingredient is the Top Ramen soup. Crunch up the noodles and throw in the spices from the little packet. Don't worry about mixing flavors (it's all good). Pour noodles and spices into a trash bag.

Now comes the fun part, start adding all the stuff you like: cans of tuna, Gringo Bandito, flavored popcorn, Crunchy Cheetos, corn chips (don't use potato chips—they'll get soggy). Basically, you throw in anything you can get when you're in prison.

Then add enough really hot water to cook the mess, tie the trash bag closed, and let it cook.

"Spread" a newspaper on a table and open up the trash bag. Everyone grabs a fork and you all stand around the spread, eating and talking about what you're in jail for.

# THAI GREEN CURRY CHICKEN

### C.J. Snare, *FireHouse*

I am a *huge* fan of Thai cuisine and was first introduced to authentic Thai food on the first of FireHouse's many tours there. From Bangkok to Khon Kaen, from Chiang Mai to Phuket, the varied foods of the regions are among the world's best at hitting all of your taste buds at once, and make for a very exciting meal. It is a very rich, exotic, and aromatic food with sweet, spicy, tropical, and sour flavors. To me, it falls somewhere between Chinese and Indian food in style and taste.

**SERVES 2**

One 13.5-ounce can coconut milk

2 or 3 tablespoons green curry paste, or to taste, as it's *hot*

1½ tablespoons creamy peanut butter

1 pound skinless, boneless chicken breasts, cut into bite-size chunks

2 tablespoons Thai fish sauce

2 tablespoons brown sugar

½ cup canned sliced bamboo shoots

½ cup frozen peas

⅓ cup chicken stock

Jalapeño chiles

Habanero chiles

Fresh basil, for garnish

Cooked jasmine rice, for serving

In a large skillet, simmer the coconut milk with the green curry and peanut butter over medium heat for 5 minutes. If you wish, start with a smaller amount of curry and add more according to taste and your spice tolerance level.

Add the chicken, fish sauce, brown sugar, bamboo shoots, peas, and chicken stock.

At this point you can choose to really spice things up by adding fresh chiles according to how much heat or spice you desire. I like to add 2 fresh jalapeños cut in thin slices, and also a small bit of fresh habanero. These chiles are optional but if you like things a little spicy, I would recommend at least one fresh jalapeño at this point.

Simmer 10 minutes, stirring occasionally. Garnish with fresh basil and serve hot over cooked jasmine rice.

# SAUSAGE BREAD

## Alan Robert, *Life of Agony/Spoiler NYC*

The winter holidays would not be the same without the smell of homemade sausage bread cooking at my mother-in-law, Joan Zagami's house. Other than drinking my father-in-law's private wine stash, devouring this sausage bread is one of the highlights for me around Christmas. My poker buds will tell you that it works great as a finger food around the game table and at Super Bowl parties as well. I would never claim to be a great chef, but my mother-in-law is! So, here's the recipe . . .

SERVES 8

1¼ pounds sweet sausage (with fennel, if preferred)
¼ cup olive oil (for frying and to brush onto bread later)
3 large onions, skinned and cut into small pieces
Salt and pepper
1 pound pizza dough

Preheat the oven to 350°F.

Remove the sausage from casing (or purchase without casing) and fry in some oil until all the pink color in the sausage is gone. Drain off the fat and set aside.

Fry the onions in a little more oil until soft and slightly brown. Add to the sausage and mix well, crushing the sausage into small pieces (crumble it with your fingers if you have to). Add salt and pepper to taste. Set aside.

Roll out the dough with a rolling pin until nice and flat, in the shape of a pizza. Spread the sausage-onion mixture evenly onto the dough (place it mostly in the center) then start at one edge and roll the dough over until it looks similar to a French baguette. Brush a coat of oil onto the bread and place onto an oiled baking sheet. Place in the oven for approximately 1 hour, until the bread is golden-brown and crusty.

Remove from the oven, slice into pieces, and enjoy!

◆◆◆◆◆◆◆◆◆◆◆◆◆◆◆◆◆◆◆◆◆◆◆◆◆◆◆◆◆◆◆◆◆◆◆◆◆◆◆◆◆◆◆◆

# BRUSSELS SPROUTS WITH CHOURIÇO SAUSAGE

## Barry Kerch, *Shinedown*

To me Brussels sprouts are the things of childhood nightmares. I was never a fan growing up but knew they were good for you. What this recipe does is make them not only palatable but amazing. Nothing like a little spicy pork and other goodies to make a nightmare a holiday dream.

**SERVES 3 OR 4**

1 pound Brussels sprouts, trimmed
1 tablespoon olive oil
½ pound chouriço sausage, roughly diced
¼ medium sweet onion, diced small
1 garlic clove, minced
¾ cup chicken stock
Salt and pepper

Bring a large pot of water to a boil. Toss in the sprouts and cook for 10 minutes. Drain and then dump in a pot of ice water. Let cool for 5 minutes, then drain again.

Meanwhile, pour the oil into a large skillet over medium heat. Add the chouriço and cook until it renders some of its fat, 2 to 3 minutes. Add the onion and garlic and cook, stirring, until the onion is very soft.

Add the Brussels sprouts to the skillet and cook for 3 minutes. Pour in the chicken stock. Reduce the liquid by half, until it thickens and begins to coat the sprouts. Season with salt and pepper and serve.

# HOT ROD PENIS LOAF

## Gen, *Genitorturers*

riginally hailing from New Mexico, I came up with this fun twist on a long-time family meatloaf dish, deciding to spice it up a bit Genitorturers-style. It has been a mainstay hit at dinner parties at our house, thanks to its kick of heat and Southwest flavor. Last time I made this, however, my husband, David "Evil D" Vincent, insisted that we alter the design in an attempt to appeal to the palates of the men folk. Thus we constructed a vagina or vulva loaf. I have to say, while it was equally tasty, the end result proved a bit disturbing and is not recommended, as the inner recesses tend to fill up with questionable-looking "juices" in a way that resembles a venereal disease. A friendly reminder of why I prefer the penis . . . bon appétit!

**SATISFIES 6 COMPLETELY!**

1 pound lean ground beef

1 pound ground pork

One can hot Ro*tel tomatoes

2 tablespoons medium New Mexico chile powder

2 celery stalks, chopped

1 small-to-medium onion, chopped

3 garlic cloves, minced or pressed

1 teaspoon whole black peppercorns

2 teaspoons cumin seeds

1 teaspoon dried oregano

½ teaspoon ground black pepper

1 egg

½ sleeve saltine crackers, smashed

2 tablespoons Worcestershire sauce (preferably Lee & Perrins)

One 8-ounce can tomato sauce or ½ cup ketchup

Preheat oven to 375°F.

Combine all the ingredients. Best way to mix is just by grabbing that big ball of meat and mashing everything together by hand.*

Once all the ingredients are well mixed, grab the entire glob and place in an ungreased 13 x 9 x 2-inch glass baking pan.

Now friends, this is where the fun begins. Fashion into the most complete likeness of your favorite penis! I prefer to make the shaft portion fairly thick. Remember, folks, it does shrink during cooking.

Bake 1 hour. Drain off excess drippings.

*NOTE: Make sure to remove any rings. Trust me on this one. It's a bad scene that will haunt you if you don't.

# SPICY TURKEY VEGETABLE CHIPOTLE CHILI

## Ron Thal, *Guns N' Roses*

**I**'m a foodie and a heat freak. When nothing is hot enough, my wife comes to the rescue with her delicious turkey and vegetable chipotle chili. It's a health-conscious take on traditional chili, with no sacrifice of flavor or fullness—loaded with fresh vegetables, and a real kick. And it tastes even better the next day.

I love cooking with my wife, but she's absolutely the brains behind the operation. I'm good for cutting vegetables and eating the ingredients before they're used, and that's about it. Here's the recipe.

**SERVES 6**

2 tablespoons canola oil

2 onions, chopped

2 yellow or red bell peppers, chopped

One 8-ounce container sliced mushrooms

1 large zucchini, chopped

1 pound ground turkey

2 tablespoons chili powder

1 tablespoon ground cumin

2 garlic cloves, finely chopped

One 7-ounce can chipotle chiles in adobo sauce, chopped (using the whole
     can will produce a very spicy chili—the way I like it. For a milder version
     use 2 or 3 peppers with a tablespoon of sauce)

One 28-ounce can crushed tomatoes

One 14-ounce can diced tomatoes with onion and garlic

One 19-ounce can dark red kidney beans, undrained

One 19-ounce can cannelini beans, undrained

1 cup dry red wine

Salt and pepper

Hot sauce (optional)

Heat the oil in a 5-quart pot. Add the onions. Sauté over medium-high heat for 2 to 3 minutes, until starting to soften. Add the peppers, mushrooms, and zucchini. Sauté, stirring occasionally, 7 to 10 minutes, until vegetables are soft and starting to brown. Transfer the vegetable mixture to a bowl and set aside.

In the same pot, brown the ground turkey over medium-high heat, stirring frequently to break up. When almost browned add the chili powder, cumin, garlic, and chipotle peppers with sauce. Cook, stirring constantly, until well mixed and heated through, about 2 minutes. Add the vegetable mixture back in and stir well. Add the crushed and diced tomatoes, kidney and cannelini beans, and the wine. Bring to a boil, then turn the heat to low and simmer for 30 minutes. Add salt, pepper, and hot sauce (if using) to taste. Can be served with cilantro, grated Colby-Jack cheese, or sour cream on top.

Enjoy!

# WEEPING BROWN EYE CHILI

## Josh Elmore, *Cattle Decapitation*

There are a lot of recipes that I enjoy, but this one always seems to get the best reaction from people whenever I fix it. I know, readers are thinking "chili, ho hum," but this zesty lava is a bit different from the normal stuff. On the surface, the recipe reads like any other veggie chili, but the addition of the cumin seeds, turmeric, cinnamon, and copious amounts of cayenne give it a distinctly Indian angle that differs from the typical American brand of chili. In my version the heat centers less on the roasted or pureed chilies and more on the combination of the cayenne, cumin, cinnamon, and turmeric.

Serve this with basmati rice if you like and enjoy cooking and eating this chili with a frosty beer of your choice. You can always add some (hail) seitan or roasted portobellos as an extra protein. Additional cayenne is always recommended.

Most people's "5-Alarm" chili is offensively not offensive. My belief is that if your nose ain't running, your lips ain't burning, your eyes ain't watering, and your mouth ain't on fire, then it ain't chili.

Sorry for all the "ain'ts," Mom.

**FEEDS AN ARMY OF HUNGRY HEADBANGERS**

1 whole bulb (head) garlic

2 to 3 tablespoons olive oil

2 teaspoons cumin seeds

2 large red onions, chopped

10 garlic cloves, finely chopped

6 serrano chiles, chopped (keep seeds)

One 28-ounce can non-chunky chamatchoes (crushed tomatoes)

One 15-ounce can tomato sauce

Three 14-ounce cans black beans, drained

Two 10.75-ounce cans condensed tomato soup

1 teaspoon salt

- 2 teaspoons ground black pepper
- 2 teaspoons dried basil
- 1 tablespoon prepared yellow mustard
- 1 heaping tablespoon chili powder
- 4 heaping tablespoons cayenne pepper (although I usually end up putting in more)
- 2 teaspoons ground turmeric
- 2 teaspoons ground cumin
- 1 small cinnamon stick
- Multiple dashes of Cholula or Tapatio hot sauce

Preheat the oven to 400°F.

Peel the outer papery skin of the garlic. Baste the garlic with a little olive oil, wrap in aluminum foil, and roast for 40 to 45 minutes.

While the garlic is roasting, pour the remaining olive oil into a large pot over medium-high heat. When the oil gets hot, add the cumin seeds. Let the seeds sizzle for a few seconds, and then add the chopped onion, chopped garlic, and serranos. Decrease the heat to medium and cook the vegetables, stirring occasionally, until the onions begin to caramelize. Remove from the heat and let cool for several minutes.

Return the pot to the burner with heat on medium and add the crushed tomatoes, tomato sauce, black beans, tomato soup, salt, and pepper. Stir occasionally for several minutes. When the mixture is combined, add the basil, mustard, chili powder, cayenne, turmeric, ground cumin, and cinnamon. Increase the heat and bring the chili to a boil.

Reduce the heat to very, very low and taste for preferred spice level. At this point I usually add more cayenne and/or the aforementioned Cholula or Tapatio. Cover the chili, still over low heat, and cook, stirring only occasionally, for at least 6 hours.

Don't forget to check the roasting garlic for doneness around 40 minutes (the cloves will be squishy). If it is completed, set aside to cool.

◆◆◆◆◆◆◆◆◆◆◆◆◆◆◆◆◆◆◆◆◆◆◆◆◆◆◆◆◆◆◆◆◆◆◆◆◆◆◆◆◆◆◆◆◆◆◆◆◆◆◆◆◆

EXTREMELY SPECIAL NOTE: DO NOT let loved ones, idiot friends, or stoned hershers peek at the chili to "see how it's doing."

After approximately 6 hours remove the chili from the heat. Let the chili cool, preferably on the stove overnight.

Reheat the chili to a simmer and add the roasted garlic by squeezing the now-pasty cloves out of their peels and into the chili. Blend in the garlic while heating through.

*Note:* Do not consume the whole cinnamon stick.

Garnish with oyster crackers, shredded cheese, yogurt or sour cream, additional cayenne, and enjoy with a hot wedge of sourdough or naan.

Find a comfortable couch and horrible TV program to watch while consuming the chili with the suggested accompaniments. Nap later.

Enjoy.

## *Suggested listening while chopping and combining ingredients*

Anaal Nathrakh—any album

The Crown—*Deathrace King*

## *Suggested listening while waiting 6 hours to eat*

Lurker of Chalice—*Lurker of Chalice*

Void of Silence—*Toward the Dusk*

Bethlehem—*Dictius Te Necare*

Burzum—*Filosofem*

◆◆◆◆◆◆◆◆◆◆◆◆◆◆◆◆◆◆◆◆◆◆◆◆◆◆◆◆◆◆◆◆◆◆◆◆◆◆◆◆◆◆◆◆◆◆◆◆◆◆◆

# CHEESE ON TOAST

## Ol Drake, *Evile*

After a hard day's work at the six strings of steel, there is nothing better (well there is, I'm just a crappy cook) than sticking some cheese on toast and blasting out some heavy metal tunes. I remember seeing Father making this legendary secret recipe, and it will be passed down through the generations of metal heads in my family, and hopefully yours, thanks to this book.

**SERVES 1**

1 brain (not to be cooked)
2 slices bread
1 block cheese

**OPTIONAL ADDITIONS**

Nails or bullets for that extra heavy metal taste
Jack Daniel's is also an interesting topping for the cheese

Put the oven broiler on full heavy metal power. Take two slices of bread. Toast one side of both pieces of the bread using the broiler.

Slice up pieces of cheese and place on the untoasted sides of the bread slices. Place on a baking sheet and throw them in the broiler. Check on them after a few minutes, or they will get very hot and burn, and that tastes bad.

Enjoy the exquisite cheese on toast!!

# BSOD BREAKFAST MASHUP

## Mike Peters, *Cancer Bats*

This is great for touring bands that don't have much money. For less than $5 a person everyone can eat a reasonably healthy breakfast! It is the most important meal of the day, after all!

SERVES 4

8 ounces veggie or meat breakfast sausage, sliced

1 tablespoon butter or margarine

1 red bell pepper, diced

1 green bell pepper, diced

1 onion, diced

One 32-ounce bag frozen hash browns

12 large eggs

Pepper

Ketchup

Hot sauce

Get the biggest frying pan you can possibly find. Everything is going into one pan!

Start by frying up the sausages as they will take the longest to cook.

Once the sausages are close to being done, add the butter, peppers, onion, and hash browns to the pan. Let those cook together for a few minutes. Add the eggs to the mix. Stir it up and cook everything over low heat for 10 to 15 minutes, or once everything looks ready to eat.

Whack a bit of black pepper, ketchup, and hot sauce on there, and your mouth is in for a treat!

# GRILLED RED ONION STEAKS

## Aaron Jellum, *Laaz Rockit*

I'm no Emeril, but if you like grilled onions on your burgers then you'll love them on your steaks as well.

Get a couple of nice rib-eye steaks and a red onion. Slice the whole onion because you will lose a few slices in the grill.

Add your steaks to your favorite marinade (I prefer "Chaka's" Mmm Sauce), and throw the onions on top of your steaks. Let sit at room temperature for about an hour before grilling.

Preheat the grill to 400°F. Grill the steaks for 4 minutes on each side. Place onions in the marinade while flipping the steaks. After each flip, place an onion on top.

Serve 'em up with your favorite cold beverage!

# MEAT AND GREED BÖRGER

## *Cripper-Brittgant Ö*

Long before thrash metal was born, a cool dude named Karl the Great with a long beard gave the order to build a chapel in the north of Germany in the year AD 810 to cultivate the heathen. This place later became known as the city of Hamburg. Who would have known that today one of the most often eaten fast foods would carry the name of that city? Even in metal, people are still arguing about the origin of the "let's-put-some-meat-between-two-slices-of-bread" idea. Some say it's an American idea, some say it must be German because of the name . . . To be honest, we don't care, but we can show you how to make a börger with style!

SERVES 4

### BÖRGER

1 red onion
1 garlic clove
1 pound ground beef
1 egg
Dry bread crumbs
Worcestershire sauce
Chili powder
Salt and pepper

### CHEESE-MUSTARD SAUCE

3½ ounces soft cheese (such as mild goat, Neufchâtel, feta, mozzarella)
½ cup crème fraîche
2½ tablespoons Dijon mustard
Salt and pepper
Chili powder
Paprika

## SANDWICH

4 burger buns
Grated cheese (your favorite)
4 frozen hash brown patties
Vegetable oil
4 slices Emmentaler or cheddar cheese
8 slices bacon
2 tomatoes
1 red onion
5 or 6 fresh mushrooms
Olive oil
1 head iceberg lettuce

### To make the börger patties

Cut the onion into small pieces. Crush the garlic, and put them together in a big bowl. Add the ground beef, egg, a handful of bread crumbs, a tablespoonful of Worcestershire sauce, and chili powder, salt, and pepper to taste. Mix it well so you get a viscid paste.

Now form four big patties. (Meat with a higher fat content shrinks during the cooking process! So be sure your raw patty is a bit larger than the bun.)

### To make the cheese-mustard sauce

Put the soft cheese, crème fraîche, mustard, and spices to taste into a bowl, mix, and that's it.

### Sandwich preparation

Heat the broiler. Cut the buns in two, coat some of the cheese-mustard sauce on the upper half, and spread some grated cheese over it. Put the cheesey buns under the broiler for a few minutes until the cheese on top is melted.

Fry the hash browns in an oiled pan or a deep-fryer until they're golden brown.

Cook the patties in a pan or a grill. When one side is ready, flip the patty, put a slice of cheese on it, and cook it until the meat is medium, well-done, or rare—depending on your taste.

Fry the bacon slices until they're crispy.

Cut the tomatoes and onion into thin slices. You may sauté the onions if you like to.

Cut the mushrooms and sauté them in a pan with olive oil until they're golden brown.

When all the ingredients are ready, it's time to complete the börger. Place a leaf of lettuce on the bottom half of the bun, so it doesn't soak up too much oil or water from the other ingredients.

Put all the ingredients (patty, hash browns, bacon, onion, tomato slices, mushrooms, and sauce) on the other half of the bun. Put it all together and tuck in!

Of course, you can customize your börger if you want to. For example, with jalapeños, fried egg, pineapple, or different dressings like barbecue or chili sauce.

# SHRIMP IN GARLIC OIL

## Johnny Kelly, *Type O Negative*

This is something that I make on the bus for the guys every once in a while. I love the taste, and it's a big hit with them. Cooking isn't something that's done all that often on a tour bus, and after being on the road for so many years I was just recently introduced to the concept. A bus is definitely different from a kitchen, and you have to improvise and make do with what's available around you. I make this dish on an electric skillet.

**SERVES 6 TO 8**

1 garlic clove, crushed
Extra virgin olive oil
2 pounds cooked, peeled large shrimp
McCormick's Montreal Steak Seasoning
Tony Chachere's Creole Seasoning
One 70-ounce package of chopped spinach
2 bags Uncle Ben's Original Long Grain Ready Rice

Set the skillet to 350°F. Brown the garlic in oil. Add the shrimp and cook for 2–3 minutes each side. Add the seasonings to taste as the shrimp are cooking. Add the spinach to the skillet.

Have your guitar player cook the bags of rice in the microwave. Add rice to the skillet. Add more Creole seasoning.

Lower heat and let simmer for about another 5 to 10 minutes.

I sometimes add garlic salt and onion powder if there's any on the bus. I make this at home with pasta instead of rice. We don't have anything on the bus to make pasta. We tried using the coffee maker once, but it didn't work out too well. Stick to rice if you're on the road!

# ROCK RAGOUT

## Markus Grosskopt, *Helloween*

This is Markus from Helloween. I've got a nice, great-tasting recipe for you right here. I call it Rock Ragout. It is based on my favorite ingredients: meat and beer! It is a very rich meal. It's heavy on calories as well, but who the hell cares? Just the way I like it. Invite friends over for some nice cold ones, listen to some cool music, and enjoy.

Cooking is very relaxing for me. Sometimes when my head is full of music, melodies, and arrangements, I go out to buy some stuff for a great meal. While cooking, I almost forget about all my stress and I start to think clearly again. Then my head is ready for some new musical adventures and challenges. Or I get very tired and I'm not able to do anything at all. So what? Tomorrow is another day. Enjoy this dish. It does me good.

**SERVES 4 HUNGRY FELLAS LIKE US**

3 pounds boneless beef, lamb, or pork shoulder or round

2 onions

Salt and pepper

Paprika

Mustard powder

Lager beer (as many as you like)

¼ pound bacon

½ pound red potatoes, peeled

½ pound carrots, peeled

½ pound green beans, trimmed

½ pound mushrooms, cleaned

1 tablespoon olive oil

4 cups heavy cream

2 to 3 tablespoons tomato paste

◆◆◆◆◆◆◆◆◆◆◆◆◆◆◆◆◆◆◆◆◆◆◆◆◆◆◆◆◆◆◆◆◆◆◆◆◆◆◆◆◆◆◆◆◆◆◆◆◆◆◆◆◆◆◆

Chop the meat into bite-size pieces. Chop 1 of the onions. Mix the meat and onion in a large bowl with salt and pepper, paprika, and mustard to taste. Now pour beer over it until thoroughly covered. Leave marinating in the fridge for 1 or 2 days.

Chop the remaining onion into bite-size pieces and set aside. Chop the bacon and set aside separately. Chop the potatoes, carrots, beans, and mushrooms and set each aside separately as well.

After marinating for at least 24 hours, drain the meat (and onions) and set aside on paper towels. Keep the beer marinade in a separate bowl for later use. Pour the olive oil in a stockpot and begin cooking the remaining (*unmarinated*) chopped onion. After half a minute, add the bacon. When bacon turns a nice golden color, add the meat mixture. Stir until browned all over.

Pour almost half of the beer marinade in the pot. Reduce the temperature so the whole dish is gently simmering for approximately an hour (depends on the kind of meat you are cooking). Add more beer marinade as it reduces.

After nearly an hour, add the green beans to the pot. After a couple of minutes, add the carrots and potatoes. Allow another 5 minutes and add the mushrooms.

Simmer for another 10 to 15 minutes. Gradually stir in the cream and tomato paste and simmer for another 2 minutes. Add some salt, pepper, and paprika to taste, and enjoy a great dish.

Cheers.

# PASTA TERROR

## Mille, *Kreator*

**m**usic while cooking: Raw Power, *Screams from the Gutter*
Invite two to three bizarros, if you don't want to eat for four!

SERVES 4

2 cups (about 10½ ounces) pine nuts

1 garlic clove, roughly chopped

¼ cup Parmigiano di bufala, grated (normal Parmigiano will do)

Large spoonful balsamic vinegar

¼ cup extra virgin olive oil

Salt

12 ounces spaghetti, penne, or whatever pasta is in the house

2 medium tomatoes, cut into small pieces

Bring a large pot of water to a boil for the pasta. Put the pine nuts in a large skillet and roast without oil until the nuts are brown, not too long!

In a food processor, combine the roasted pine nuts, garlic, Parmigiano, balsamic vinegar, olive oil, and a pinch of salt and pepper. Process until a smooth paste forms, adding more olive oil if necessary.

Salt the water, and add the pasta. Cook until the pasta is al dente. Drain the pasta, and mix with the pesto. Toss with the tomatoes, sprinkle with pepper, and serve with some red wine.

Jeff Pilson (Dokken/Dio) with his "Rock 'N' Rolly Guacamole." (COURTESY OF RAVINDER PILSON)

Claudio and Chondra Sanchez (Coheed and Cambria) show off their "Nacho Pie." (COURTESY OF JENNIFER PARK)

Chris Letchford (Scale the Summit), making "Summit Salsa." (COURTESY OF LOUIE HEREDIA)

Athon, with members from Black Tusk, cooking up "Grilled Shrimp." (COURTESY OF CHRIS "SCARY" ADAMS)

Jeff Paulick, with members from Lazarus A.D., serving "Thrash Kebabs." (COURTESY OF OLIVIA DECHIARA)

John Alaia (Moth Eater) and his "Metal Mushroom Tuna Melt." (COURTESY OF ALYSSA ALAIA)

Jeremy Thompson (Nashville Pussy), "Remo's Hot, Sweet, and Sticky Ass-Kicking Wings." (COURTESY OF NATALIE HAMBY)

Ash Pearson (3 Inches of Blood), prepping for "The Heavy Stew." (COURTESY OF ASH PEARSON)

Keri Kelli (Alice Cooper), noshing on some "BBQ Grilled Pizza." (COURTESY OF GREG GARCIA)

C. J. Snare (FireHouse) presents his "Thai Green Curry Chicken." (COURTESY OF BRENDA SNARE)

Barry Kerch (Shinedown) and his "Brussels Sprouts with Chouriço Sausage." (COURTESY OF LORI KERCH)

Ol Drake (Evile), mesmerized by his "Cheese on Toast." (COURTESY OF HIS MOM, JUNE DRAKE)

Mike Peters and his fellow Cancer Bats bang out a "Bsod Breakfast Mashup." (COURTESY OF MARK NOODLE)

Guillaume Bideau (Mnemic) throws together "The Hell Wok." (COURTESY OF GUILLAUME BIDEAU)

Frankie Banali (Quiet Riot/W.A.S.P.), "Linguine and Clams Castellamare." (COURTESY OF REGINA RUSSELL)

Brock Lindow (36 Crazyfists) rocks out with some "Reindeer Sausage and Pasta." (COURTESY OF CARRIE LINDOW)

Dave Witte (Municipal Waste), "Turkey Gyoza with Soy-Vinegar Sauce." (COURTESY OF AMY MCFADDEN)

Jackie Chambers and members of Girlschool whip up a "Motorheadbangers Hangover Pie." (COURTESY OF SINGH LOW)

Felix Hanemann (Zebra) checks on his "Roasted Turkey Dinner." (COURTESY OF ARTIST)

Jan Kuehnemund (Vixen) presents "Jan's Jammin' Simple Salmon." (COURTESY OF JAN KUEHNEMUND)

Nathan "N8 Feet Under" Garnette (Skeletonwitch) throws together some "Silver Turtles." (COURTESY OF SCOTT HEDRICK)

Mitch Lucker (Suicide Silence) stirs up some "Jerk Chicken." (COURTESY OF JOLIE LUCKER)

Joey Vera (Fates Warning) serves up his "Grilled Mushroom Pizza." (COURTESY OF TRACY VERA)

Dan Lorenzo (Hades/Non-Fiction) and the key ingredients for "The Dish." (COURTESY OF GINA LORENZO)

Page Hamilton (Helmet), concentrating on his "Halibut."
(COURTESY OF JENNY PARK)

Jed Simon (Tenet/Strapping Young Lad) shows us how it's done with his "White Wine and Garlic Pasta."
(COURTESY OF SUSANNA KRAMER)

Max Cavalera (Soulfly/Sepultura), grilling up "Brazilian Lemon Chicken."
(COURTESY OF GLORIA CAVALERA)

Timmy St. Amour and members of Howl devour "Thai-Style Red Curry." (COURTESY OF ANDREW FLADEBOE)

John Bush (Armored Saint), cookin' up some "Trailer Park Shepherd's Pie" on family night. (COURTESY OF DOLLIE SILVERA)

Tim "Ripper" Owens (Judas Priest), "Grilled Pizza." (COURTESY OF JEAN OWENS)

Boys' night in with Blaze Bayley and members of Iron Maiden, "Sausage Curry." (COURTESY OF ANDREW EAMES–TRIPLE A IMAGE UK)

John Ricco (Warrior Soul), "Busted Chops." (COURTESY OF CHERILYN CARKHUFF)

Jason Decay (Cauldron), "Welfare Wedges." (COURTESY OF JASON DECAY)

Joey Z (Life of Agony) introduces the guests of honor for his "Stuffed Lobster Zampella." (COURTESY OF FAMILY MEMBER)

Matthew Bachand (Shadows Fall) and "The Stuffing Within." (COURTESY OF LISA JOY)

Erik Larson (Alabama Thunderpussy), cooking "Drunk Touring Band Mush." (COURTESY OF HIS WIFE, CHRIS BOARTS LARSON)

John Bundy and his Naam bandmates taste test his "Pecan Pie." (COURTESY OF DOUGLAS GRAHAM)

Steve Blaze (Lillian Axe) and sous chef as they prepare "Death by Chocolate." (COURTESY OF JULIE NUNENMACHER)

Chef Dave Ellefson (Megadeth/F5), "Star Cookies" and "No-Bake Cookies." (COURTESY OF DAVE ELLEFSON)

Ron Thal (Guns N' Roses) and his wife stir up some "Spicy Turkey Vegetable Chipotle Chili."
(COURTESY OF THE RON THAL)

Mike Meselsohn (Black Water Rising), cooking a "Rockin' Cheese Omelet."
(COURTESY OF HIS WIFE, JERMAINE GERENA)

C.J. (The Wildhearts), "Seafood Linguine."
(COURTESY OF C.J)

George Lynch (Dokken),
"Shrimp Pesto Fettuccine."
(COURTESY OF DANICA LYNCH)

Alan Tecchio (Autumn Hour/Non-Fiction/Hades)
reveals his secret ingredient for "Chicken à la Al."
(COURTESY OF BETH TECCHIO)

Danny Leal (Upon a Burning Body),
"Danny's BBQ." (COURTESY OF
DANNY LEAL)

Jeremy "Jerms" Genske (Dirge Within) presents his "Deviled Chicken." (COURTESY OF THE BAND)

J.C. (Danko Jones), enjoying his "Calabrian-Style Stuffed Eggplant." (COURTESY OF MARINA CALABRESE)

Diamond Dave Ardolina (Moth Eater) rocking the "Shrimp and Pasta with Broccoli." (COURTESY OF CHRISTY ARDOLINA)

◆◆◆◆◆◆◆◆◆◆◆◆◆◆◆◆◆◆◆◆◆◆◆◆◆◆◆◆◆◆◆◆◆◆◆◆◆◆◆◆◆◆◆◆◆◆◆◆

# RIDICULOUSLY DELICIOUS BEER BRATS

### Robert "Rawrb" Kersey, *Psychostick*

I accidentally came across this little recipe from a few friends for Super Bowl parties and such. I did some refinement and tried experimenting with different beers and different types of brats. That said, you can mix and match beers and brats to your own, unique liking. I'm definitely not a chef, so if I can do it, anyone can. Enjoy!

SERVES 12

2 red onions
3 tablespoons butter
4 large bottles beer (24 to 40 ounces)
12 bratwursts
12 hot dog buns
Mustard

Chop the onions into medium strips. Place in large frying pan with the butter. Put over medium heat. Pour beer into large stockpot and place over medium-high heat.

Sauté the onions in the butter until they're brown and soft. Once the beer is boiling, add the onions. Remove the brats from the packaging and place them into the boiling beer. Boil for 5 to 10 minutes, until the brats are a grayish white.

Preheat the grill to 400°F. Drain the brats and onions and place on the grill, turning until brown. Be careful not to pierce or cut the brats because you will lose all of the yummy juices. Serve in hot dog buns. Best with mustard.

# SICILIAN (RASTA) METAL MEATBALLS

## James Farwell, *Bison bc*

**T**his recipe was inspired by my good friend Mike Campitelli, drummer for the Sorcerers, reggae sk8 punk, and all-around Italian Stallion.

**SERVES 4**

Olive oil

1 garlic clove, finely chopped

1 large shallot, finely chopped

Salt and pepper

Two 28-ounce cans whole plum tomatoes

One 6-ounce can tomato paste

Brown sugar

Beer (Old Milwaukee, Rainier, Old Style Pilsner, PBR—nothing with too much flavor)

1 pound ground lean bison

1 pound ground lean pork

1 egg

½ fistful of fine dry bread crumbs

1 fistful of fresh basil leaves, ripped to shreds

1 fistful of pine nuts

1 fistful of golden raisins

1 fistful of grated Parmesan cheese

12 ounces egg noodles

### Getting the sauce did

In a medium pot add ½ cup olive oil, 1 garlic clove, the shallot, and salt and pepper to taste. Set over low heat and cook until soft, stirring often.

In a bowl, combine the tomatoes and manually mutilate with bare hands. Add the mutilated tomatoes to the pot and set to medium heat.

After the sauce comes to a boil, add the tomato paste and brown sugar to taste. Give it a good stir and boil it at medium heat. (As a rule I usually add salt and a sip of beer to each stage of cooking.)

◆◆◆◆◆◆◆◆◆◆◆◆◆◆◆◆◆◆◆◆◆◆◆◆◆◆◆◆◆◆◆◆◆◆◆◆◆◆◆◆◆◆◆◆◆◆◆◆ ◆

## Getting the balls did

In a good-size bowl, combine the bison, pork, egg, bread crumbs, salt and pepper to taste, basil, pine nuts, raisins, Parmesan, and 1 shot of olive oil.

With your bare hands, mash the shit out of it until blended consistently, all the while trying not to get any of your greasy hair or shitty face pubes in it. Then cover the meat with a towel, have a smoke, and pound a beer.

To make balls, take a tablespoon of mutilated meat concoction, cup it between two hands while gently caressing and rolling it until it is formed to the likeness of your own balls, or of the balls of a loved one.

Place the balls in a dry frying pan. Set over medium-low heat and cover. Cook until dark on all sides (this will take about 30 minutes), pouring beer over the meatballs once or twice as they cook. Don't flood the meatballs with beer, just soak them in a nice little bath.

Once meatballs are cooked, pour a generous portion of the tomato sauce into the pan to soak up the grease and escaped pine nuts. Set to simmer.

While meatballs are simmering, bring a large pot of water to a rolling boil, adding a shot of oil and salt. Add the pasta of your choosing. I prefer egg noodles, but it is really up to you.

Once pasta is done, drain and toss with the sauce and meatballs.

◆◆◆◆◆◆◆◆◆◆◆◆◆◆◆◆◆◆◆◆◆◆◆◆◆◆◆◆◆◆◆◆◆◆◆◆◆◆◆◆◆◆◆◆◆◆◆◆◆◆◆◆◆

# SPAGHETTI BOLOGNESE

## Steve Grimmett, *Grim Reaper*

Spaghetti Bolognese is my favorite meal because it is very homey, and it warms the old cockles on those cold and wet English days (believe me, there's a lot of them!). Also, it is very easy to make. If I can make it, then anyone can!

SERVES 2

½ pound lean ground beef
1 package gravy mix (I use Gravy Granules here in the UK)
1 onion, finely chopped
⅔ cup canned tomato sauce
One 14-ounce can diced tomatoes
Worcestershire sauce
Salt and pepper
6 ounces spaghetti

Get a large saucepan on medium heat. Add your lean ground beef and cook until browned. For extra taste, sprinkle and stir in some gravy mix.

Add the onion and cook for 2 to 3 minutes, until softened. Stir in the tomato sauce until the beef and onion are covered. Add the tomatoes and stir. Add a few drops of Worcestershire sauce. Season with salt and pepper to taste. Stir. Reduce the heat and simmer for 15 to 20 minutes.

Meanwhile, in a medium saucepan, boil salted water. Add the spaghetti. Bring to a boil. Reduce the heat and simmer for 10 to 12 minutes, until cooked. Drain the spaghetti and serve with the Bolognese sauce over the top. ENJOY!

# METAL MEAT LOGS

## Bill Gaal, *Nothingface*

Here's one that Tom Maxwell and I used to cook up the morning after a long night of drinking.

**SERVES 4 TO 8**

1 onion

3 pounds ground beef

1 tablespoon garlic salt

2 cups vegetable oil

One 12-ounce package egg roll wrappers

First, you need to start with a nice hangover and an upset stomach. It sets the mood.

Next, you dice up the onion really fine. Then you throw it in a pan with your ground beef. Throw in your garlic salt, and fry it up, savoring the greasy steam that is filling your nose.

While that is cooking, pour the vegetable oil into a pot. Heat the oil over medium heat.

After the meat is finished cooking and has turned a beautiful shade of dark brown, remove from heat and allow to cool.

Next, lay your egg roll wrappers out on the counter, fill them with your meat (mm-mmmm . . . ), and follow the instruction on the packaging to wrap them properly. This works best as a two-man operation. One filling the wrappers, the other rolling them up.

When you have all of your meat logs wrapped, you can then begin deep-frying them. Put a couple of rolls into the hot oil, cooking them until the wrappers are golden brown. Then remove them from the oil with tongs and drain on a paper towel.

By the time you're done, you'll have enough greasy, delicious metal meat logs to give your entire band a heart attack!

# THE HELL WOK

## Guillaume Bideau, *Mnemic*

Simply because in the band, some of us are jalapeño lovers and *all* of us love hot spices. This recipe allows you to prepare it as you wish. Not that hot, super hot, or hot as hell!

Plus, this dish is pretty advantageous because of all the vegetables. It's high in protein, high in vegetables and vitamins, and low in fat. It fills your stomach but it's really low in calories. It's perfect for when we come back from tour looking like fat elephants. See what I mean? Heh, heh.

**SERVES 2**

2 ounces Chinese black mushrooms

Boiling water

1 big red bell pepper

2 big red onions

4 carrots

Olive oil

Balsamic vinegar

5 ounces water

1 pound skinless, boneless chicken breasts

½ cup sour cream

Chopped parsley

8 garlic cloves, crushed

Salt and pepper

In the end you can also add jalapeños, Tabasco sauce, or any other fire-spitting spices you like to make it brutal and heavy!!!

First, soak the Chinese black mushrooms for 20 minutes in some boiling water. Once this is done, place them under cold water and then finely slice them. Set aside for later.

Slice the bell pepper, onions, and carrots finely.

Plunge the carrots in salty boiling water for approximately 4 or 5 minutes. They must remain crunchy so you'll taste them better as the cooking goes. Once they're cooked, rinse them quickly under cold water and set aside for later.

Fry the onions and pepper in olive oil in a frying pan. Add 3 or 4 tablespoons of balsamic vinegar and 5 ounces water. Let the whole thing boil until the water is gone, but don't let the whole thing burn . . . or the roof, by the way!

Chop your chicken in approximately 1-inch cubes. Fry them in 2 tablespoons olive oil in a frying pan. Don't cook them too much; they must remain tender.

Once the chicken is cooked, grab a wok or a big pan and put the carrots, onions, peppers, chicken, and mushrooms in it with 2 teaspoons olive oil and 3 tablespoons balsamic vinegar. Cook the whole thing on low heat.

Add the sour cream, as much parsley as you want, and the garlic. Add salt and pepper to suit your taste.

Mix the whole thing and in 5 minutes, you can serve!

# MEATLOAF AND MEATBALLS

## John Petrucci, *Dream Theater*

T his is one of my favorite recipes because it's so easy to make, and everyone loves it! Even Meat Loaf himself won't be able to resist my meatloaf!

**SERVES 6**

1 pound ground beef or a combination of ground beef, pork, and veal

3 eggs

1½ cups Progresso Bread Crumbs, Italian Style

½ cup grated Romano cheese

2 tablespoons olive oil

½ teaspoon garlic powder

Salt and pepper

One 14-ounce can of low-sodium chicken broth

Preheat the oven to 350°F.

Mix together the beef, eggs, bread crumbs, cheese, oil, garlic powder, and salt and pepper to taste with clean hands in a large bowl. Press into a loaf pan. Pour the chicken broth over the top of the meatloaf until covered. Bake for about 1 to 1½ hours until a meat thermometer reads 160°F.

## MEATBALLS

Same basic meatloaf recipe. Just shape into meatballs and fry in olive oil until cooked thoroughly.

# LINGUINE AND CLAMS CASTELLAMARE

## Frankie Banali, *Quiet Riot/W.A.S.P.*

**T**his recipe, originated in Castellamare del Golfo, Sicily, was a favorite of my father and handed down by example.

**SERVES 4**

½ cup extra virgin olive oil
1 pound local, wild mushrooms or small portobellos, stems discarded
8 garlic cloves, diced
Red pepper flakes (I like a lot of it!)
1 cup pinot grigio or other dry white Italian wine
5 pounds littleneck clams
1 pound fresh linguine
Sea salt and coarsely ground black pepper
Shaved Romano cheese

Heat ¼ cup of the olive oil in a large, heavy, deep skillet over high heat. Add the mushrooms, and sauté until they begin to brown. Using a slotted or draining spoon, remove the mushrooms to a plate.

Add the remaining olive oil and the garlic to the pan. Sauté until the garlic is soft but not brown. Add the red pepper flakes, wine, and clams. Cover and cook until clams open up, roughly 6 to 8 minutes. (Throw away any clams that did not open during the cooking process because this means that nature put a hit on them . . . Atsa no good!)

While the clams are cooking, cook the linguine in a large pot of salted, boiling water. (When cooking the pasta, try not to overcook—pasta should be a little firm.) Drain the pasta completely and place in a large bowl. Spoon mushrooms over the linguine, then top with the clam mixture. Season with salt, pepper, and an ample supply of shaved Romano cheese. A true family favorite!

# HUNTER-STYLE WESTPHALIAN SAVOY ROULADES

## Tom Angelripper, *Sodom*

The meat of a wild boar is a rare commodity and has a naturally low fat content. Since not everybody is a hunter, or knows one, the roulades can also be prepared using customary ground pork or ground beef. But this—for sure—is only half the treat. Larger portions can easily be done on a baking sheet and frozen without any problems.

Fluffy potatoes boiled in broth or mashed potatoes go well with the roulades. I wish all of the readers much delight trying this recipe! See you all! Cheers!

SERVES 4

1 day-old bread roll, torn into pieces
2¼ cups venison stock (if possible homemade, but also of quite good quality available in a jar)
1 pound ground wild boar meat
2 green onions (scallions)
1 red bell pepper
Olive oil
1 egg
2 tablespoons hot prepared English mustard such as Coleman's (which I first tried on tour from an English catering service—excellent!)

1 teaspoon paprika
Salt and freshly ground pepper
Fresh or dried thyme
1 medium savoy cabbage
7 tablespoons butter
1 Spanish onion
1 thick slice bacon
1 cup red wine
½ cup sour cream
1 little bunch parsley, finely chopped

Put the torn bread and 1 cup of stock in a small bowl to soften. Gently squeeze out any excess liquid, but leave the bread nice and moist.

Place the ground meat and soaked bread in a bowl. Dice the green onions and red pepper. Heat a small amount of oil in a skillet over medium-high heat. Add the onions and bell pepper and cook, stirring, to brown slightly. Add ¼ cup stock, reduce the heat to medium, and cook until they become translucent. Let them cool down a bit and transfer to the bowl with the ground meat and bread. Add the egg, mustard, paprika, and salt, pepper, and thyme to taste and mix thoroughly with your hands. Season to taste. Cover, place in the fridge, and let sit for about 30 minutes.

Take eight huge leaves off the savoy cabbage, cut out the ribs, and blanch them in boiling water. Let them cool and pat dry with a paper towel. Finely chop the rest of the cabbage and add to the ground meat mixture.

Stack two cabbage leaves and fill with one-fourth of the meat mixture. Roll up carefully like a burrito. Tie with twine or special fastener. Make sure the ends of the roulades are tight, so that no meat juice leaks. Repeat until you have four tightly rolled roulades.

Preheat the oven to 375°F.

Put the roulades in a huge skillet and sear in the butter. After that, transfer the roulades to a roasting pan and roast in the oven for 1 hour. Baste the roulades every once in a while with the stock.

Finely chop the Spanish onion, dice the bacon, and sauté together gently in a skillet until they are golden brown. Quench with red wine and the remaining 1 cup stock until reduced, while stirring in the sour cream bit by bit. Add the parsley, then decant the gravy into a small saucepan and keep warm.

Take the savoy roulades out of the roasting pan and cover to keep warm. Add the meat juice from the bottom of the roasting pan to the gravy. Add seasoning if necessary, and cook until it begins to boil.

Serve with red wine, or—as a matter of course—a chilled glass of Diebels Alt.

# DANNY'S BBQ

## Danny Leal, *Upon a Burning Body*

This is a recipe for some tasty, down-home, easy-to-make Texas BBQ, and it's one of my favorites! Two of the ingredients are household products that are very common and inexpensive. Everyone gives their big recipes with secret this and secret that. This one is from me to you for all the people who just want a super good li'l taste of Texas BBQ, and they want it yesterday. :) Hope you enjoy!

Charcoal grill must be at a very low flame—not too much fire coming off the coals.

Cut 1 large white onion (you need 1 onion for every 2 people) in half and wrap each half separately in foil. Place in the back of the grill over indirect heat, away from the fire. Do this about 30 minutes before you start cooking up your chicken. Flip and rotate onions about every 15 minutes. When done, unwrap foil, soak the onions with lemon juice, and season with lemon pepper. Let sit for 5 minutes before eating.

Season each piece of chicken (I always use chicken leg quarters from the local meat market. They come in bags of 9 to 10 pieces.) with 1 teaspoon honey, 1 teaspoon lemon pepper, cayenne pepper to your own liking and will, and ½ teaspoon Mrs. Dash.

Place the chicken on the grill. When the chicken starts to pop open a li'l bit, I like to fill um up with a little beer! Adds to the taste.

Let the chicken cook for about 30 to 40 minutes, but eyeball and flip them every 3 to 5 minutes. You know it is done when you cut a little slit and sneak a peek. If you see pink or blood then you have to give it more time. No pink then you are ready to rock. It takes practice to get your timing right and your chicken perfect.

# DEVILED CHICKEN

## Jeremy "Jerms" Genske, *Dirge Within*

I f you eat a lot of chicken and are looking for a new twist, this recipe is quick and easy. What makes this chicken devilish (other than the chef!) is the sauce adapted from ingredients used to make deviled eggs. Deviled chicken goes great with any family-style side and even better with a cold beer!

**SERVES 2 TO 6**

2 to 6 skinless boneless chicken breast halves, trimmed*

4 tablespoons (½ stick) butter, melted

1 tablespoon lemon juice

1 tablespoon prepared yellow mustard

1 teaspoon salt

1 teaspoon paprika

¼ teaspoon ground pepper

Preheat the oven to 375°F.

Place trimmed chicken breasts in a glass casserole dish. Combine all the other ingredients and pour over the top of the chicken. Bake for 30 minutes, basting halfway through.

Serve immediately, and make sure you spoon excess sauce over the top!

* Depending on how saucy you want your Deviled Chicken, you can choose how many chicken breasts to use. We like it saucy . . . so we use two.

# TURKEY GYOZA WITH SOY-VINEGAR SAUCE

## Dave Witte, *Municipal Waste*

**T**his is a pretty easy meal, and I make it quite often for bands staying at my house. It makes for a fun group meal and is pretty healthy. I put a twist on traditional pork gyoza and use turkey instead. My favorite part is the assembly. I love having a drink or two while listening to music and chatting about touring while folding the dumplings into form.

### MAKES 50 TO 60 DUMPLINGS, PERFECT FOR ANY HUNGRY TOURING BAND

#### SAUCE

½ cup soy sauce

½ cup rice vinegar

1 tablespoon brown sugar

1 green onion (scallion), finely chopped

#### GYOZA

2 tablespoons soy sauce

2 teaspoons grated fresh ginger

1 teaspoon brown sugar

4 garlic cloves, minced

1 pound ground turkey

2 cups chopped fresh spinach

1 green onion (scallion), finely chopped

1 package dumpling wrappers (available in any Asian market)

2 tablespoons vegetable oil

*To make the sauce*

Combine all the ingredients in a small bowl. Set aside.

## To make the gyoza

Mix the soy sauce, ginger, brown sugar, and garlic in a large bowl. Add the turkey, spinach, and green onion. Mix well and set aside.

Spoon about 2 teaspoons of filling in the center of each wrapper. Moisten the round edge of each wrapper with water. Fold wrapper in half and press round ends together. Fold 3 small pleats in the joined ends of the wrapper.

Boil the gyoza until they start to float. Pull the gyoza out, drain off the water, and transfer to a skillet. Fry in the oil until each side is brown. Remove from pan and drain on paper towels. Serve with the sauce.

# MOTÖRHEADBANGERS' HANGOVER PIE

## Jackie Chambers, *Girlschool*

*There was a young girl from Leeds*
*Who knew how to satisfy greed*
*She'd pile up her plate*
*She ate and she ate*
*'Til finally she had to concede (Bum Bum!)*

**B**eing a Yorkshire girl, I grew up on a staple diet of meat and two veg, huge helpings, bread with every meal, and a healthy appetite for anything even slightly edible, not too good for the hips but wonderful passing my lips! Sunday lunch would always start with a few Yorkshire puddings swimming in lashings of onion gravy, then a main dish, and of course a sweet pudding. Yes, we eat well in Yorkshire. It's cold! We'd eat a lot of shepherd's pie, as it's easy to make, pretty cheap, and doesn't take too long, and it's very filling when you have the Yorkshire puddings with it.

Not being the greatest cook in the world—and I'm sure there's a few survivors who would testify to that—whenever I have friends over, instead of panicking about what to order in (I mean, cook), I say to myself, "I'm going to M.I.L.F. it" (Make It Like Father's), and it can't go wrong.

So here's his recipe (with a little of my metal influence thrown in for good measure). Enjoy!

P.S. Any stomach or general complaint, my dad's name is Colin, and he still lives in Leeds.

**SERVES 4 PEOPLE OR 2 VERY HUNGOVER ONES!**

### YORKSHIRE PUDDINGS

Vegetable oil

2 large eggs

1 cup milk

1 cup all-purpose flour

1 teaspoon salt

One 16-ounce bottle Grolsch beer

## PIE

| | |
|---|---|
| 1½ pounds potatoes (or double for extra mosh) | Thyme |
| | Salt and pepper |
| 1½ pounds lean ground lamb or beef | 2 tablespoons milk |
| 1 large onion | 4 tablespoons (½ stick) butter |
| 1 cup beef broth | 2 baby carrots |
| Rosemary | |

So *LEMMY* show you how to make a stodging hangover meal of *MotörHEAD*bangers shepherd's pie with Yorkshire puddings. Firstly, turn the oven on so hot that Satan himself would need to wear oven gloves, then pour some oil into each cup of a muffin tin. Place the tin in the oven to heat.

Whilst it's smoking nicely, mix the eggs, milk, flour and the (veruca) *SALT*, whisk like a *DEMON* and go (*zakk*) *WYLDE* to get as much *AERosmith* in there as possible, then add the secret ingredient us Yorkshire folk add, a Sp*LASH* of (*dave*) *GROHL*sch beer. After you add the beer, down the rest. Hair of the dog, hangover sorted? Now to sort out the stodge part to start all over again.

Open the oven and pour the mixture into the muffin tin. You'll need to *RUSH* this a bit, as the oven has been heated to an *EXTREME* heat. If you don't get the oil hot enough, then the puddings will sink and be as heavy as *LED* (*Zepellin*). Place in the oven and turn the heat down to about 350°F *AC* (*DC*) and bake for about 20 minutes, or until the puddings rise. Don't open the oven *DOOR*(s) or they will sink. Be careful taking out the tin as it (*brian*) *MAY* be very hot!

Next, (*john*) *PEEL* the potatoes and put them on to boil keeping your eyes *CLAPTON* on them so that they don't get too mushy.

Meanwhile, in a frying pan (*paul*) *COOK* the (*tommy*) *LEEn* ground meat until it's almost *BLACK SABBATH*ed then *CUIT* the onion and *CHUCK BERRY*thing in the pan to simmer, stirring in the broth with a (*ronnie*) *WOODe*n spoon, then add a (*uriah*) *HEEP*ed spoonful of rosemary and thyme and a little (*gary*) *MOORE* salt and pepper to taste.

◆◆◆◆◆◆◆◆◆◆◆◆◆◆◆◆◆◆◆◆◆◆◆◆◆◆◆◆◆◆◆◆◆◆◆◆◆◆◆◆◆◆◆◆◆◆◆◆

Mosh the potatoes with a *METALlica* mosher and with as much *VENOM* as possible, using a *LITTLE* (richard) milk and lots of butter to make sure they're very *CREAMy*! Place the meat mixture into a very *DEEP* (purple) dish and then start to add a *sCOOPER* at a time of the moshed potatoes on top of it. Then, using a fork, make a few (white) *STRIPES* across the potatoes.

Finally, (*iggy*) *POP* the pie (*jeff*) *BECK* into the oven under the broiler to brown the surface. When it's browned *aMUSE* yourself and (*zz*) *TOP* off your pie by adding 2 carrots as horns. Dish up the meal, but let it *girlsChOOL* down a little bit.

Please be aware that this meal could lead to a little (hawk) *WIND* but be assured that no *MSG* was used during the (*ginger*) *BAKERing* of this recipe.

# REINDEER SAUSAGE AND PASTA

### Brock Lindow, *36 Crazyfists*

Reindeer sausage is a staple item in almost every Alaskan home. Lots of people just cut it up and serve it with cheese and crackers. I wanted to do something a little different. I love making spaghetti, and have a couple other money spaghetti recipes. This one gets the highest marks, though. It's great to make ahead of time for camping trips, or after a long day of fishing. I love this recipe because it's spicy and hearty—the way the reindeer sausage melds with the marinara gives it a unique flavor—almost a little barbequey.

**SERVES 4 TO 6**

8 ounces spicy Alaskan reindeer sausage
8 ounces plain Alaskan reindeer sausage
Olive oil
1 medium white or sweet onion, chopped
1 pound mushrooms, sliced
Sea salt
16 ounces angel hair pasta
One 16-ounce jar marinara sauce
Sriracha hot chili sauce
Grated Parmesan cheese

Slice the sausages into ½-inch slices.

In a large skillet, pour a little olive oil and start browning the sausage slices over medium-high heat. Add the onions and sauté with the sausage. Add the mushrooms and sauté for a minute or so. Turn down the heat to medium-low.

Boil some water, add olive oil and sea salt, and cook angel hair pasta for 4–6 minutes or until al dente.

Add the marinara sauce to the skillet. Add Sriracha sauce to taste (HOT!).

Drain the pasta and add to the skillet. Sprinkle top with Parmesan cheese and serve.

Serve with Marietta Old Vine Lot 49 red wine, garlic bread, and a green salad.

++++++++++++++++++++++++++++++++++++++++++++++++++++++++++++

# CALABRIAN-STYLE STUFFED EGGPLANT

## JC, *Danko Jones*

**m**y grandma used to make this for me when I was a kid, and it always brings back memories of being at her house in Calabria. Since she is no longer around, I had to learn how to make it on my own. Serve with a nice bottle of red (preferably southern Italian). It makes for one of the best main courses you could have. Hope you enjoy.

**SERVES 4 TO 6**

6 small eggplants

1 bread roll

½ cup milk

½ onion

1 small red hot pepper, such as peperoncino

Extra-virgin olive oil

Salt

1½ cups tomato sauce

1 pound ground beef

Finely chopped parsley

5 ounces grated Parmesan

5 ounces grated pecorino cheese

1½ cups dry bread crumbs

2 eggs

Preheat the oven to 250°F.

Cook the eggplants in boiling water for 15 minutes. Drain eggplants. Cut them in half, scoop out the inside, and finely chop the meat of the eggplant.

Place the bread roll in a small bowl and soak it in the milk. Let sit.

Finely chop the onion and the hot pepper. Sauté them with olive oil and salt. Add the tomato sauce and ground beef. Stir and keep over low heat for about 5 minutes. Stir in some parsley.

In a bowl, mix together the chopped eggplant, Parmesan, pecorino, bread crumbs, milky bread roll (torn into pieces), and the eggs.

Fill each eggplant half with the mixture and put in a large baking dish. Pour the tomato/beef sauce over each half.

Bake for 30 to 45 minutes.

Serve lukewarm.

◆◆◆◆◆◆◆◆◆◆◆◆◆◆◆◆◆◆◆◆◆◆◆◆◆◆◆◆◆◆◆◆◆◆◆◆◆◆◆◆◆◆◆◆◆◆◆◆◆◆◆◆◆◆

# SHRIMP PESTO FETTUCCINE

## George Lynch, *Dokken*

This recipe came to me from my mom, Barbara, who lives a very simple, healthy, bohemian lifestyle; well read and well traveled . . . traveling off the beaten path, so to speak, who in turn, passed it on to my wife, Danica, a few years ago. Danica was going through a transformation in her eating habits and wanted to cook healthier meals for us and our children, and this recipe was both healthy and delicious. Its ingredients come from mixed sources. It has elements of Mediterranean, Asian, and Italian cooking. And some of the ingredients are considered aphrodisiacs . . . especially the asparagus. Bonus!

**SERVES 4**

8 ounces whole-wheat fettuccine

1 pound asparagus, trimmed and cut into 1-inch pieces (4 cups)

½ cup sliced jarred roasted red and yellow peppers

⅔ cup sliced green onion (scallion)

½ cup prepared pesto

1 tablespoon red pepper flakes

2 teaspoons olive oil

1 pound peeled and deveined shrimp

1 teaspoon minced garlic

1 cup dry white wine

Ground pepper

Bring a large pot of water to a boil. Add the fettuccine and cook for 3 minutes—less than the time indicated on the package. Add the asparagus and continue cooking until the pasta and asparagus are tender, about 3 minutes more. Drain the fettuccine and asparagus and return to the pot. Stir in peppers, green onions, pesto, and red pepper flakes. Cover to keep warm.

Heat the oil in a large skillet over medium heat. Add the shrimp and garlic and cook about 3 minutes. Add the wine, increase the heat to high, and continue cooking until the shrimp are curled and the wine is reduced, about 5 minutes. Add the shrimp to the pasta, toss, season with pepper, and serve.

◆◆◆◆◆◆◆◆◆◆◆◆◆◆◆◆◆◆◆◆◆◆◆◆◆◆◆◆◆◆◆◆◆◆◆◆◆◆◆◆◆◆◆◆◆◆◆

# ROCKIN' CHEESE OMELET

## Mike Meselsohn, *Black Water Rising*

I'm not really great in the kitchen but I've always been good with eggs, and I enjoy making and eating omelets. It's pretty quick and easy to do, and there are so many variations to keep it fun and interesting. I prefer cheddar, but you can try different cheeses like American, Swiss, Monterey Jack, etc. You can also add veggies, meat, fruit, or basically anything edible you want to put in there. After a hard night of partying, there's nothing better to eat in the morning than a hot, buttery omelet oozing with cheesy goodness!

SERVES 2, OR 1 HUNGRY MAN

4 large eggs
2 tablespoons water
2 teaspoons butter
2 ounces cheddar cheese (or any type you like),
    shredded or thinly sliced
Salt and pepper

Get a 10-inch nonstick pan very hot over medium heat. Whisk together the eggs with the water.

Add the butter to the pan. When butter melts, add the egg mixture. Push or lift the edges into center to allow uncooked egg to reach the pan. When the egg is set, add the cheese. Add a dash of salt and pepper.

When the cheese melts, fold over in half and place on a plate.

Eat and enjoy!

# MAMA NUDO'S TORTELLINI A LA ROSE

## Vince Nudo, *Priestess*

**T**here are a few things in this world that work as glue to keep the Priestess brothers tight: our music, our van, and food. As band member Mikey Heppner remembers, "When Vince first invited us over for a dinner at his parents' house in St. Leonard, none of us could have imagined the bond that was about to form over a special pasta dish, a pasta dish that would be the new yardstick by which all other pasta dishes would be measured. Oh the hard nights of starvation, being forced into shitty ass Subway restaurants, where we would have sacrificed our souls for this pasta dish! This dish is Mama Nudo's Tortellini a la Rose. Now your life can truly begin."

**SERVES 4 TO 6**

½ pound pancetta
5 tablespoons olive oil
1 cup sliced mushrooms
Salt
1 large onion
1 garlic clove
2 tablespoons brandy
1 pound fresh ripe tomatoes (preferably plum tomatoes), skin and seeds removed, *or* 1½ cups drained canned tomatoes, preferably imported Italian, drained, *or* ¾ cup homemade tomato sauce if you are fortunate enough to have some
Red pepper flakes (optional)
Two 20-ounce or four 9-ounce packages fresh cheese-filled tortellini, or frozen
Freshly ground black pepper
1 cup heavy cream
Freshly grated Parmigiano
Chopped parsley, leaves only

Cut the pancetta into small pieces. Put in a medium frying pan and cook very slowly for about 10 minutes, until crisp and golden. Drain the excess oil and set the pancetta aside on a paper towel–lined plate.

Heat some of the oil in the frying pan and add the mushrooms along with salt to taste. Sauté until soft and golden, about 6 minutes. Set the mushrooms aside.

Finely chop the onion and garlic. Heat some oil in a saucepan. Add the onion and garlic along with salt and cook gently until golden, about 10 minutes.

Add the brandy and let it evaporate. Add the tomatoes along with the reserved pancetta and the mushrooms and red pepper flakes to taste (if using), and simmer very lightly for 20 minutes, until sauce is completely cooked and thick.

To cook the tortellini, fill a stockpot with a large amount of cold water, and place on high heat. When the water reaches a boil, add salt to taste. Add the tortellini to the boiling water a few at a time. Fresh tortellini will cook in 2 to 3 minutes, whereas frozen can take a few minutes longer. Test them to insure they do not overcook.

Taste sauce for salt and pepper, and stir in cream. Cook for 5 minutes longer. Once the tortellini are cooked, remove them with a strainer or skimmer. Reduce heat under the saucepan to very low and add the tortellini. With a large metal spoon, carefully mix very well. Remove from heat and let stand for a few minutes to allow sauce to homogenize.

Garnish with grated Parmigiano and chopped parsley and serve.

# ROASTED TURKEY DINNER

### Felix Hanemann, *Zebra*

**T**he reason I like to cook and serve this recipe is simple. I have kids, and I'm originally from New Orleans. So I love New Orleans–style food. Red beans and rice, gumbo, jambalaya, you name it. However, kids don't generally like those types of foods. So I started cooking foods that I know that they like and are also healthy. I call it "combat cooking," or cooking clean. Meaning that you do what you have to do to make something work.

This recipe has all-natural ingredients. Fresh turkey or chicken, real mashed potatoes, and fresh string beans or haricort verts. This recipe is an excellent base with which to cook many other dishes. Many of the ingredients can be exchanged for other foods. For example, you can use broccoli instead of string beans. You can use an 8-pound chicken instead of a turkey or turkey breast and you can either make baked potatoes or sweet potatoes if you don't want to make mashed potatoes. It's basic cooking, but you can add cranberry sauce with it, or use stuffing for the turkey, add a salad and dessert, and you have a really nice meal. I've cooked this meal for many of my friends and relatives, and it always hits the spot. I hope everyone enjoys this recipe as much as I do. Enjoy!

**SERVES 6**

6- to 8-pound turkey breast (preferably
    Shady Brook Farms—fresh is better;
    thaw if frozen)
Salt and pepper
Onion powder
Garlic powder
1 small onion

Honey
Real maple syrup
5 decent-sized russet (baking)
    potatoes
Milk
Butter
1½ pounds fresh green beans

Preheat the oven to 375°F.

Rinse the turkey breast in the sink. Still in the sink, liberally shake salt, pepper, onion powder, and garlic powder all over the turkey. Put the turkey in a roasting pan (disposable is easier than cleaning a real dish, but if you do use a real pan, line it with aluminum foil to help keep it clean). Slice up the onion and place in the roasting pan with the turkey and about 2 cups of water.

Place the pan in the oven and set a timer for 2 hours. Remember to baste it. After about 90 minutes, coat the turkey with honey and maple syrup, and then baste it again with the turkey juices that accumulated in the bottom of the pan. Cook for at least another 30 to 45 minutes, until a meat thermometer registers 165°F, or the "popper" pops.

While the turkey is cooking, peel and slice the potatoes and place them in a big pot of boiling water. Don't start boiling them until after the turkey has been cooking for 90 minutes. Once the potatoes are soft, empty out the water and add salt, garlic powder, about ½ cup milk, and ⅓ stick butter. Begin to mash them together with an old-fashioned masher, then use an electric mixer to really whip them up.

Start boiling the green beans after you have started the mashed potatoes. I usually cut the tips off both ends. Green beans should only be boiled for 12 to 18 minutes. Empty the water and rinse the beans once they are done. Add salt, garlic powder, and about 4 pats of butter to taste.

A beautiful Roasted Turkey Dinner with real mashed potatoes and fresh green beans in 2 to 2½ hours. Your friends will love it and of course it doesn't hurt to have a little wine while cooking the dinner and be sure to pick up a nice dessert. Enjoy!

# SILVER TURTLES

## Scott Hedrick, *Skeletonwitch*

Like true sons of midwestern darkness, Skeletonwitch likes to camp and barbeque. A lot. While some bands might get a hotel on their day off, we almost exclusively find a campground, a bunch of beers, some firewood, and some delicious grillables. To quote the mighty Satyricon, "The Forest Is Our Throne," err, hotel.

This is a recipe for "silver turtles." We like to make these because they are delicious and simple. Silver turtles require minimal tools, and the ingredients can be bought on the cheap. Essentially almost any combination of ingredients can be used to make a silver turtle. You could make it Mexican themed, Asian, Polish, or whatever strikes your fancy. Let's begin.

**PER PERSON**

  1 medium-large potato
  ¼ onion
  ¼ bell pepper
  ½ carrot
  2 tablespoons butter or garlic butter
  ½ cup sliced mushrooms
  1 or 2 hamburger patties (this can be substituted with almost anything:
    fish, sausage, chicken, etc.)
  Salt and pepper

Build a campfire (you could use a grill, but that isn't nearly as fun).

Cut up the potato, onion, bell pepper, and carrot however you prefer, but be careful not to cut the potato too thick, as it will not cook well. Lay out a piece of aluminum foil about 18 inches long. Spread butter on the foil and then place your veggies (mushrooms, too) on top of the buttered area. Next, place your meat on the top and salt and pepper to taste (we've also considered adding taco sauce, barbecue sauce, teriyaki, hot sauce, etc.).

To complete the preparation process, wrap the concoction two to three times in the aluminum foil, alternating directions so none of your goodies can leak out and nothing undesirable can get in.

Once the fire has burned down to coals, place your silver turtle package into the fire. If you have a camp shovel, you can cover the top of the bundle in coals; if not, you'll have to flip the turtle once about halfway through the cooking process. Let the turtle sit in the fire for 45 minutes.

Once the turtle is cooked, pull it out of the fire and carefully unwrap it. Add condiments of your choosing (ketchup and mustard work great), crack a beer, and enjoy.

# JAN'S JAMMIN' SIMPLE SALMON

## Jan Kuehnemund, *Vixen*

**T**his is my favorite recipe for several reasons. First, I absolutely love salmon. Second, this recipe for the salmon marinade is quick and easy to put together, and the end result (I think!) is quite tasty! :) I like the hint of Asian flavor that comes from the ginger, toasted sesame oil, and soy sauce. Third, if there's ever any of the grilled salmon left over, it makes a great addition to any green salad for lunch the next day! And last but not least, (wild) salmon is a healthy choice and is sooo good for you!!!

FEEDS 4

**MARINADE**

1 cup orange juice

¼ cup extra virgin olive oil

1 tablespoon toasted sesame oil

3 tablespoons lite soy sauce

2 garlic cloves, finely chopped

4 green onions (scallions), finely chopped

2 teaspoons finely grated peeled fresh ginger

1 tablespoon brown sugar


4 wild Alaskan salmon fillets or salmon steaks

Olive or canola oil


Combine the orange juice, olive oil, toasted sesame oil, soy sauce, garlic, green onions, ginger, and brown sugar in a medium bowl, and stir together.

Place the salmon in a shallow baking dish and pour the marinade over the salmon, carefully turning to coat both sides. Chill and marinate for 30 to 45 minutes (or less if you're in a hurry!).

◆◆◆◆◆◆◆◆◆◆◆◆◆◆◆◆◆◆◆◆◆◆◆◆◆◆◆◆◆◆◆◆◆◆◆◆◆◆◆◆◆◆◆◆◆◆◆◆◆◆◆◆◆

Preheat the grill to 300°F. Lightly brush the grill grates with a little olive or canola oil.

Remove the salmon from the marinade (put the marinade aside) and place salmon on the grill. Grill for 4 to 5 minutes per side, turning only once (start with skin side down, if salmon still has skin on).

If you will be cooking inside, I recommend "grilling" the salmon on a pancake griddle or similar pan on the stove. Spray a little cooking spray, plus a few drops of toasted sesame oil on the griddle, before turning the heat on to medium to medium-high. Grill salmon on griddle for 4 to 5 minutes per side, adjusting heat as necessary.

Heat the reserved marinade in a small saucepan on the stove to almost boiling, and lightly drizzle over salmon before serving.

Serve salmon with your favorite side dishes! I recommend a small dinner salad of mixed greens, tomatoes, and mushrooms with olive oil and vinegar dressing, sprinkled with chopped walnuts and seasoned with herbs, such as rosemary, garlic powder, and freshly ground pepper.

My other favorite sides with this (along with the salad) are brown rice, flavored with lite soy sauce, and steamed broccoli or grilled zucchini or corn on the cob!

Enjoy! :)

# SALMON ON AN OPEN FIRE

## Mathias Nygard, *Turisas*

I don't really cook at home, but when out in the wild woods I just love cooking! Fresh ingredients, preferably hunted or picked, and the slightly ascetic circumstances make everything so enjoyable and exciting. This is a very simple recipe, and there's nothing better than sitting by an open fire on a summer evening watching your fish slowly cook while you sip from your bottle and listen to the sounds of nature. You can see me preparing this dish on our 2008 DVD release, *A Finnish Summer with Turisas*.

Preparations: 2–3 hours

> Salmon fillet(s) (about ½ pound per person)
> Sea salt
> Butter

I would not recommend trying to prepare this dish in your apartment, but rather somewhere outside. The basic idea is that the salmon fillets are nailed to a plank and will slowly cook *next* to the open fire—not in or on it. Also, make sure the weather conditions are right. If it's windy outside, the required mild and even heat from the fire will be thrown around by the breeze.

Spread out the fillets and rub some salt in them. You can use quite a lot of salt, especially if you're using big-grained sea salt (which I think is the best). Note that thicker parts of the fish need a bit more salt. No other spice or seasoning is really needed. If you want, you can add some lemon pepper (a seasoning mix consisting of 20 to 40 percent salt, black or white pepper, and dried lemon skin), but go very easy on it and remember that the seasoning also includes salt. It's extremely easy to completely lose the great taste of fish with spices. Set aside the fillets for a couple of hours while they absorb the salt.

◆◆◆◆◆◆◆◆◆◆◆◆◆◆◆◆◆◆◆◆◆◆◆◆◆◆◆◆◆◆◆◆◆◆◆◆◆◆◆◆◆◆◆◆◆◆◆◆◆◆◆◆◆◆◆◆

Next you'll need to set up a fire. Use proper firewood, not half-wet spruce that will only result in thick smoke and sparks and ash flying into your meal. Then you'll need planks that will fit one or two fillets each. Alder is best, but you can use any hardwood that can take the heat. If you end up going a bit punk rock and using just whatever construction planks happen to be around, make sure they are not treated with any chemicals, as you wouldn't want to have that in your fish. Luckily you can get away with almost anything if you cover the plank with aluminum foil. This might also be a good idea if you think you might be reusing the plank at another time.

After the fillets have had their couple of hours with the salt, toss off any visible excess grains (can be a bit nasty to chew on). Nail the fillets to the planks, skin side down, using wooden nails of pinky-finger thickness, cut out of birch branches. Use your knife to cut a small hole through the skin and into the wooden plank underneath it and then nail in the wooden stick to keep the fish in place. You'll need four to eight nails to make it work. Make sure the sticks are nailed sturdily into the plank, otherwise you might end up having ash-baked salmon.

Melt some butter in a pot and brush it on the surface of the fillets. The hardcore way to do it is with juniper branches, but if you're in a more urban environment, there are quite a few modern-day solutions for this.

Now it's time to place the fish planks *next to* the fire, preferably a spot close to the fire yet far enough that you won't burn your hands (usually 10 to 30 inches from the flames). You can place the planks upright or lying down—just try to look for a spot where the whole plank will get about the same amount of heat. Also note that you might need to turn and move the planks around a bit during the cooking process due to wind changes and because the fish will cook unevenly anyway as thinner parts cook faster than thicker parts. The simplest way to get the planks standing up facing the fire is by leaning them against stones. Again, make sure they don't tip over.

The cooking will take at least 45 minutes, during which the fire should be kept alive and steady by adding more wood as needed. Be careful not to stir up too much ash flying around when doing this. Brush on some more butter every now and then to keep the fish moist. Note that there will be a lot of grease dripping off the fish, so if your fire pit is anything more than a hole in the ground out in the woods, it might be a good idea to cover up your design patio with aluminum foil.

Use a fork or your knife to determine doneness. When the salmon is evenly colored and the thickest part next to the skin doesn't appear raw, it's ready.

The fish is best served straight off the planks with boiled potatoes, fresh green salad, and cold beer, vodka, or white wine—if there's any left after waiting for the fish to cook!

# JERK CHICKEN

## Mitch Lucker, *Suicide Silence*

I swear by this chicken because I love super hot, bold-tasting food with a lot of flavor. This chicken soaks it up like a sponge (hint: that's why you poke so many holes in it). So grab a 6-pack of your favorite beer because it goes perfectly with chicken and enjoy!

SERVES 4

### SPICE RUB

2 teaspoons habanero chile sauce

3 tablespoons chopped onion

2 teaspoons dried thyme leaves

6 tablespoons sugar

3 teaspoons ground nutmeg

1 tablespoon salt

4 teaspoons Tabasco sauce

4 or 5 skinless, boneless chicken breast halves

1 tablespoon butter

Mix together all the spice rub ingredients in a big bowl. Poke a lot of holes in the chicken pieces with forks, or what I do is bundle up a bunch of wooden skewers and go at it. Make sure there are plenty of holes on both sides of the breasts. Put them in the spice rub and turn to completely coat the chicken breasts. Marinate for 1 hour in the fridge.

Put the butter in a large skillet and place over medium to high heat. Place the chicken breasts (and the onions) in the skillet and cook for 6 or 7 minutes per side. Make sure all the onions are caramelized.

Serve with rice and green beans. That's how I do it! It's a delight!

◆◆◆◆◆◆◆◆◆◆◆◆◆◆◆◆◆◆◆◆◆◆◆◆◆◆◆◆◆◆◆◆◆◆◆◆◆◆◆◆◆◆◆◆◆◆◆◆

# GRANDMA'S NORWEGIAN STEW

## John Nymann, *Y&T*

This was my grandmother's recipe, which she handed down to my mom. This was my favorite meal when I was a kid. I still love it and make it for my family. There are many variations of this dish in Norway, but this one rocks! Easy to make with no added salt or seasonings.

SERVES 4

2 pounds corned beef

2 celery stalks

8 carrots, peeled

2 rutabagas, peeled

8 white potatoes

1 large onion

1 large green bell pepper

½ head of cabbage

Chopped fresh parsley (optional)

Rinse the corned beef, place in a large pot, and put enough water to just cover the meat. Bring the water to a boil, then reduce heat to low and cover. Cook for 3 hours.

Chop the celery, carrots, rutabagas, potatoes, and onion into ½-inch cubes.

Once the meat is fully cooked and very tender, remove it from the pot and set aside. *Do not* pour out the water that the beef was cooked in. Place all the chopped veggies in the corned beef stock and bring to a boil. (Do not add more water.) Reduce the heat to low and cover.

Chop the cabbage into wedges and add to the pot after the vegetables have simmered for an hour. Chop the corned beef and throw it back into the pot and cook for 30 more minutes.

Sprinkle chopped parsley, if desired, on top. There you have it . . . enjoy!

# THE DISH

### Dan Lorenzo, *Hades/Non Fiction*

I love The Dish because it is easy to make and tastes great . . . plus it has the colors of the Italian flag!

SERVES 3 OR 4

2½ quarts chicken stock

1 ball wet mozzarella, about 1 pound (if it's not wet, forget it!)

4 medium to large tomatoes (ugly/vine-ripe, or even better, New Jersey garden)

1 large handful fresh basil leaves (not the silly, dry kind)

1 pound penne or rigatoni

The best extra virgin olive oil you can find

½ teaspoon sea salt

I call this recipe "The Dish" because it's easy and delicious, and I don't have a real name for it. I don't eat any meat at all, but I will use chicken stock to boil the pasta for this meal. That being said, get out a pot and heat up the chicken stock until it boils. While you're doing this, get out a large bowl. Cut up the wet mozzarella into bite-size pieces (take it out of the refrigerator an hour before you start The Dish). Cut the tomatoes into bite-size pieces. Rinse the basil and tear the leaves in half or more to bring out the flavor.

Cook the pasta until it's at the desired softness. While you're boiling your pasta, put the tomatoes, basil, and mozzarella into the bowl and toss together. Get out a colander and drain off most, but not all, of the chicken stock. Pour the cooked pasta and some stock into the bowl with the tomato, basil, and mozzarella. Drizzle some extra virgin olive oil and add sea salt to taste, stir, and serve. See? I told you it was easy!

# GRILLED MUSHROOM PIZZA

### Joey Vera, *Fates Warning*

**I**f you live in a suburb like I do, there's rarely a great place to get a pizza. And I live in a Los Angeles suburb, for chrissakes! My choices are either some soggy delivery joint where a pimply-faced punk brings me a greasy and overly salty mess, or I have to drive to my local "Italian" restaurant which around here has more in common with Signore Chuck E Formaggio than anything remotely Italian. Sure, I can make a trip down to the city and savor a rustic pie from Mario Batali's Mozza Pizzeria, and believe me it's worth it, but I don't always have the time. So I like to make my own outside on my grill!

I make my own pizza dough and sauce. If you're too busy, or making your own dough seems like a disaster waiting to happen (it won't be, it's so easy), then by all means use your favorite sauce from a jar and a premade pizza dough from your local deli. I've been known to take such a shortcut in my culinary travels, too, so don't feel like a chump. But the difference is jaw dropping when you make your own shit from scratch. Read on.

About the sauce and dough: my sauce recipe is a variation on a sauce that was taught to me from my best friend's father, who grew up in what was then the predominantly Italian neighborhood of Boyle Heights in 1940s Los Angeles. His name was Mr. Bush, and I use this recipe as a basis for all my tomato-based sauces. It's great on pizza but also any kind of pasta dish, so refrigerate the leftovers and mangia tutto!

The dough recipe is pretty much borrowed from Mario Batali, and it is a simple and quick, no-frills pizza dough. It can be used for a variety of flatbread recipes also. Slather some Nutella on it, I don't care. Just try it. You won't regret it.

**SERVES 4 TO 6**

### THINGS YOU'LL NEED

Large bowls

Wooden spoon

Kitchen timer (optional)

Dish towel, clean

Sauté pan

Dutch oven or saucepan

Immersion blender or canister blender

Pizza stone

Metal spatula (optional)

Pizza peel (uh, big giant paddle-looking thing made out of wood)

Gas grill

## PIZZA DOUGH (MAKES FOUR 12" PIZZAS)

¼ cup white wine, at room temperature

¾ cup warm water

1½ ounces dry active yeast

1 tablespoon honey or sugar

1 tablespoon extra virgin olive oil

1 teaspoon kosher salt

3 cups all-purpose flour, sifted, plus more for dusting

Cornmeal, for dusting

Oil

## MUSHROOM TOPPING

Extra virgin olive oil

8 ounces crimini mushrooms, sliced thick

8 ounces oyster or chanterelle mushrooms, sliced thick

1 teaspoon fresh thyme leaves

Kosher salt and freshly ground pepper

## SAUCE

Extra virgin olive oil

1 onion, diced

1 carrot, peeled and diced

Kosher salt

1 garlic clove, minced

One 28-ounce can of whole plum tomatoes, emptied into a large bowl with juices and crushed with your hand

½ teaspoon sugar

1 cup grated fresh mozzarella

1 cup grated fontina or Asiago

+++++++++++++++++++++++++++++++++++++++++++++++++++++++

*Make the Pizza Dough*

In a large bowl combine the wine, water, and yeast. With a wooden spoon, stir well until all yeast is dissolved. Add the honey, olive oil, and salt and stir to combine. Add 1 cup of the flour and mix until you make a smooth batter. Add the remaining 2 cups of flour and stir until most of the flour is incorporated. Then use your hands and pull the dough out of the bowl and place on a flour-dusted work surface. You can't cheat here. Knead it for about 8 minutes and it will become smooth and elastic. Use a timer if you have to.

After this, put the ball of dough into a very lightly oiled large bowl, and with your fingers rub a little of the oil all around the dough ball. This keeps a skin from forming. Cover with a dish towel and leave bowl in a warm spot in your kitchen for 45 minutes. The dough will rise to twice its size.

While you're waiting, make some sauce and mushroom topping. You can do this the day before too, no problem! The use of two different kinds of mushrooms and cheese here makes a much more interesting pie. So don't get lazy on me!

*Mushroom Topping*

Heat a large sauté pan over medium-high heat. When the pan is good and hot, add enough olive oil to coat the bottom of the pan. Add the mushrooms so they cover the bottom of the pan and don't stir for 3 minutes! We're going for a sear and color right away, so don't touch it for 3 minutes! If your pan is not big enough, do this in two batches. You don't want the mushrooms to sit in layers because they will steam rather than sear.

After 3 minutes, add the thyme and salt and pepper to taste, then stir and continue to sauté for another 5 minutes or until you see good coverage of golden brown on most of the mushrooms. Remove from the pan and set aside.

*Sauce*

Heat a medium Dutch oven or large saucepan on medium heat. When the pan is hot, add enough olive oil to coat the bottom of the pan. Add the onion and carrot and a pinch of salt. (The salt helps draw water out of the vegetables. After some evaporation, they will sauté.) After 5 minutes or so, add the garlic and sauté another minute, taking care to not let the garlic turn brown. Add the tomatoes, including their liquid, and add another pinch of salt. Bring up to a simmer and cook about 10 minutes.

Add the sugar, stir, and check if you need more salt. Add it if you think so! Remove from the heat and insert an immersion blender and blend until smooth. (If using a regular blender, only fill halfway and keep lid ajar to let steam escape. If you don't, the heat will expand and your lid, along with most of your sauce, will end up on your kitchen ceiling!) Check for final seasoning (salt), and sauce is done.

*Let's Make Some Pizza*

Place the pizza dough on the flour-dusted surface and cut into four equal pieces. Knead each piece for 30 seconds while forming into a small ball. Place the four balls of dough on a lightly oiled cookie sheet or large plate. Cover again with a dish towel and let rise again for 15 minutes. After this, the dough is done and ready to make your pizzas.

In my opinion, to make a great pizza at home, it has to be cooked on a pizza stone. Get one.

Place your stone right on top of the gas grill, off to one side, and fire up that bad boy on full. You'll need the grill to be blasting at about 600°F to get a good pie. Preheat it until you get that high temp (10 to 20 minutes) and then turn down the fire to low on the side where the stone is. Leave the other side at high. This is similar to indirect cooking. That's right, just like a wood-burning oven.

Take your pizza peel and lightly dust it first with a little bit of flour. Spread it around and shake off any excess into your sink. Then dust the peel with a little cornmeal and spread evenly. This step helps your pie slide right off the peel and onto the pizza stone. Without this step, your dough may stick to the peel and the only things that go flying off into the fire are your toppings!

Take one ball of dough and place it on a flour-dusted surface. With your fingers and palms, flatten the dough so it resembles a circle, flipping it over a few times while doing it. Don't worry about making it perfect, it should *look* homemade, after all! You should be able to make it roughly 12 inches or so in what would resemble a diameter. And it should be no more than ⅛-inch thick.

Put the dough on your pizza peel, add only 1 to 2 tablespoons of your sauce, and spread evenly. Don't use more than this, *please*. You only need a little sauce for a good pizza. Top with some of the mozzarella and fontina (again, not too much) and then some of the mushrooms.

## To the Fire!

Put the peel toward the rear of the stone and with short, quick motions, pull the peel toward you, allowing the pizza to slide off onto the stone. Slide that guy right onto the fiery pizza stone and close the lid. Check after 5 minutes, and if one side seems to be cooking faster or is slightly burning, go in and rotate your pie so it cooks evenly. Close the lid and check back after another 3 minutes. The cheese and outer crust should look lightly browned. Total cooking time should be 7 to 10 minutes, depending on how hot your grill is. Remove it using your peel (you may need a metal spatula to slightly lift the pie so you can get the peel under it) and let rest about 2 minutes before slicing up.

Looks good, doesn't it? Now open a decent bottle of any Italian red wine and make the other three pizzas!

✦✦✦✦✦✦✦✦✦✦✦✦✦✦✦✦✦✦✦✦✦✦✦✦✦✦✦✦✦✦✦✦✦✦✦✦✦✦✦✦✦✦✦

# HALIBUT

## Page Hamilton, *Helmet*

I don't get too fancy when I cook, and don't really follow instructions well—which is why I'm in a rock band and not out stumbling around making a mess in the real world. I was up in Alaska as a judge for the Warped Tour Battle of the Bands earlier this year and got to go deep-sea fishing as part of my compensation. We caught halibut, cod, and rock fish, and I brought a bunch of halibut home with me. Since I was dating this chef from The CIA (not the intelligence agency but the culinary school) at the time, I asked her to help me cook this fish right cuz I had already wrecked a bunch of it. It's good. I like it. Yeah, man.

This is more of a method of preparing halibut than a recipe, but, whatever. It's damned good.

**SERVES 4**

3 tablespoons olive oil
2 large lemons
1½ pounds skinless halibut fillets
Salt and pepper
Fresh basil leaves

Heat the olive oil in a large skillet on high heat. While you're doing this, squeeze half a lemon on each side of the halibut in a dish and season well with salt and pepper.

Put the fillets in the oil for about 3 minutes, until the fish no longer sticks to the pan.

Flip the fish and squeeze the rest of your lemons on it. Keep the burner on high for 2 more minutes and then lower heat to medium-low and continue cooking until fish is firm and cooked all the way through.

Chop up the fresh basil and sprinkle it on top and eat.

◆◆◆◆◆◆◆◆◆◆◆◆◆◆◆◆◆◆◆◆◆◆◆◆◆◆◆◆◆◆◆◆◆◆◆◆◆◆◆◆◆◆◆◆◆◆◆◆◆◆◆

# BULGOGI

## Rick Wartell, *Trouble*

I chose this recipe mainly because it was the first thing I learned to cook when I was around fourteen or so. My sister made it for me one evening after having it at a girlfriend's house, who just happened to be Korean. I loved it so much I had her teach me how to make it for myself so that I could enjoy it as often as I wanted. I have tried many varieties and variations on the recipe since then and am convinced the one I submit here is by far the best way to make a perfect bulgogi.

**SERVES 2 TO 4**

1 pound round steak (or any boneless cut)
½ cup soy sauce
1 tablespoon sesame oil
3 garlic cloves, chopped
3 tablespoons sugar
2 tablespoons chopped fresh ginger
Sesame seeds
Black pepper
Shot of white wine
Chopped scallions (green onions), for garnish

Partially freeze the meat. This will make it easy to slice very thin.

Combine the remaining ingredients (except scallions) in a large bowl. Add the sliced meat. Marinate at room temp for 1 hour or refrigerate overnight.

Fire up that grill to super hot. Grill meat high for about 1 minute per side. Serve over rice and garnish with chopped scallions.

Serve with sake, cold beer, or both.

# WHITE WINE AND GARLIC PASTA

## Jed Simon, *Strapping Young Lad/Tenet*

This is one of my faves. Just make sure you eat it with someone else, so neither of you can smell each other's garlic breath. It's a great meal by itself, but goes perfectly with vegetables, grilled meat, etc., too. The amounts listed below are approximate. Adjust according to your preference.

**SERVES 2**

¼ cup olive oil

2 tablespoons butter

1 medium white or yellow sweet onion

Salt and freshly cracked or ground pepper

Spices—oregano, Italian seasoning, ground cumin, onion powder, garlic powder

One 750ml bottle of white wine (a low- to mid-priced pinot grigio or chardonnay works fine for cooking . . . and guzzling)

5 large garlic cloves

5 fresh vine or Roma (plum) tomatoes, finely diced (a 14.5-ounce can of diced tomatoes is okay in a pinch)

One 12-ounce package egg fettuccine

One 15-ounce jar Alfredo sauce (optional)

Chicken breast, shrimp, lobster etc. (optional)

Chopped fresh basil leaves

Freshly grated Parmesan cheese

Ready? Let's roll.

Get your olive oil and butter heating up over medium-low heat in a large sauté or frying pan.

Dice the onion, get it in the oil-butter and cook until onion is translucent (for you word-challenged people, that means clear or see-through); 8 to 10 minutes will do it. While the onion is cooking, add some salt, some pepper, some spices and some of that wine (more on the wine below). The spice thing is a personal choice, so use what you like. I use a lot of everything.

I use about a half bottle of that wine in my sauce. You'll want to add some while the onion cooks, let it simmer and cook off, and then add some more. That way you get the flavor of the wine into the base ingredients, which is tasty. The rest of the bottle of wine goes into my stomach while I'm cooking. You should do the same.

Mince the garlic and add to the onions when they are nearly done. Gently mix it all together and simmer for not more than 1 minute. Nothing ruins shit faster than overcooked garlic. Seriously. If ya wanna get all fancy, then finely slice the garlic by hand rather than mince it. It's a better flavor and not quite so intense as when minced.

Okay, so let's add the diced tomatoes, mix 'em in and let simmer over medium heat until the tomatoes are cooked down and soft, about 10 minutes. While this is happening it's a good time to add more wine to the pan, and to your stomach. Hell, have a beer, too. Start adding more spice and keep tasting it until you are happy with it. Like I said, spice is a personal thing, so you do what you like, okay? Okay. Now is a good time for a vodka and tonic.

So let's turn that heat down to a low simmer. Done? Okay. Keep your eye on it and stir it every now and then. If it looks like it's getting too thick, add some wine.

Get your other big pot full of water and get that thing boiling, 10 minutes or so. Add the noodles, some salt, and stir. Another 12 minutes or so, and you are done with the pasta. Drain and keep in the strainer until ready to use.

With me so far? Good.

You could eat it as is right now, and it would be freakin tasty, I assure you, but let's say you want to bulk it up a bit. This is where you can add a jar of your favorite Alfredo sauce to the tomato mixture. Yep, good ol' bottled sauce . . . dump that thing right into the tomato and onion base and let it heat up a bit more. Voilà! Instant creamy tomato sauce, and DAMN is it good!!! I could tell you here how to make Alfredo sauce from scratch, and it's awesome, but I just use the bottled stuff most of the time, and it rocks, so why get complicated?

Wanna bulk it up even more? Marinate some skinless, boneless chicken breasts in olive oil, lemon, and garlic, and then grill those babies up nicely. Add them to your finished pasta and you got good eats. You can also use shrimp, or lobster . . . That's why I like this recipe so much. It's great by itself, but killer if you add a little cooked flesh to the mix.

So go over to the strainer, get some pasta out, add a little olive oil, and toss if it's a bit sticky, and pile that shit high on your plate. Add a generous helping of the sauce, some freshly chopped basil on top, as much freshly grated Parmesan as you like, cracked or ground pepper, some chicken or fish if you decided on that, and you are on your way to a fine, food-induced coma. Beautiful.

Enjoy!

Oh, I also find that cooking while playing guitar keeps me relaxed and in the zone. If you don't play guitar, then try cooking to the Tenet album. That gets the juices flowing nicely!!

# BRAZILIAN LEMON CHICKEN

## Max Cavalera, *Soulfly/Sepultura*

**B**BQing outside w/ favorite jams on the boom box. First make sure you have a full tank of propane for the grill. When I go to the store, I always look for the fattest chicken drumsticks that I can find. And the key is the fresh lemons. They flavor the BBQ chicken all the way through.

> Chicken (I usually use thighs and drumsticks)
> Lemons
> Olive oil
> Garlic, minced
> Fresh rosemary (optional)
> Barbecue sauce (optional)
> Salt

The main ingredient here is a big dash of maniacal metal. This is a must. While I am going through my CDs, looking for something tantalizing, the chicken legs are soaking in a plastic zipper bag, along with olive oil, freshly squeezed lemons, and a bit of garlic. Sometimes I throw in some fresh rosemary. The longer the chicken soaks, the juicier and more tender it will be.

Preheat the grill to 400°F. Take the chicken out of the bag and place on the heated grill. Take the juice from the bag and baste the legs while they are cooking. Squeeze additional fresh lemons over the chicken. Do this several times. I usually coat half the chicken in barbecue sauce. Serve up with a lot of salt.

# WHIPLASH SHRIMP CREOLE

## Tony Portaro, *Whiplash*

The Whiplash Shrimp Creole has been a longtime favorite of the band. The shrimp tastes awesome in the spicy sauce with an ice cold beer. Make it extra hot and tasty with papaya-habanero–based Last Nail in the Coffin hot sauce, or go for the burn using Power and Pain. The rat race of the tristate area doesn't leave time for much else, so this recipe not only tastes great, but it's easy to throw together. You can even save time by buying cooked shrimp that's ready to eat . . . it'll give you more time to thrash!

**SERVES 2**

1 medium onion, finely chopped
2 tablespoons butter or margarine
1 medium green bell pepper, chopped
¼ cup chopped celery
1 bay leaf, crushed
1 teaspoon salt
1 teaspoon chopped parsley

At least ¼ teaspoon cayenne pepper (more if desired)
One 6-ounce can tomato paste
2 cups water
1½ to 2 pounds cooked shrimp
Hot steamed rice, for serving
Whiplash Hot Sauce of your choice*

*Order from www.frommildtowild.com

In a skillet, cook the onion in the butter until tender. Stir in everything else but the shrimp, rice, and hot sauce. Cook over low heat, stirring occasionally, for 30 minutes. Stir in the shrimp until all is well heated. Serve over rice. Add your favorite Whiplash Hot Sauce.

# TRAILER PARK SHEPHERD'S PIE

## John Bush, *Armored Saint*

SERVES 4

1 small onion, chopped
14 tablespoons (1¾ sticks) butter
1½ pounds ground beef
Two 8-ounce cans tomato sauce
1½ cups frozen mixed vegetables, thawed (or substitute any
    vegetables of your choice)
One 40-ounce beer
Salt and freshly ground black pepper
8 to 10 medium red-skinned potatoes
1½ cups milk
½ cup sour cream
1¼ cups grated mozzarella cheese
Garlic powder
2 cups biscuit mix
1 cup freshly grated Parmesan cheese
¼ cup french-fried onions (any brand) or bread crumbs
Nonstick cooking spray

### Beef Layer

Sauté the onion in 2 tablespoons of the butter. Add the ground beef. After the beef is browned, add tomato sauce and mixed vegetables. Add ¼ cup beer. Add salt and pepper to taste.

### Potato Layer

Peel and slice potatoes ¼-inch thick. Cook in boiling water for approximately 15 minutes or until fork-tender. Drain. Whip the potatoes with electric mixer; mix until moderately smooth. Do not overbeat; a bit lumpy can be good. Heat and add ½ cup of the milk, followed by 1 whole stick butter, the sour cream, and the mozzarella. Add salt, pepper, and garlic powder to taste. Whip until mixed. Adjust thickness by adding more milk, if desired.

## Biscuit Layer

Combine the biscuit mix and the remaining 1 cup milk. The mix should be thinner than normal biscuit mix but not runny.

In a separate bowl, mix the Parmesan and the french-fried onions. Set aside.

Turn on the generator. Light the pilot on the trailer home oven. Preheat the oven to 350°F.

Spray a 9 by 13-inch baking pan, or similar casserole with cooking spray. Layer with the mashed potatoes. Spread the meat–mixed vegetables on top. Pour the biscuit batter over the meat. Melt the remaining 4 tablespoons butter and drizzle over the top.

Bake for 30 to 40 minutes, until the top is golden brown.

Sprinkle the Parmesan-onion mixture over the top and bake for 5 minutes more until cheese is melted and starting to brown and crisp (altitude may vary cooking time).

If sober, drink the remainder of the beer.

# THAI-STYLE RED CURRY

## Timmy St. Amour, *Howl*

I chose this recipe not only because it is one of my personal favorites, but because it has become my staple dish to cook for friends throughout the years. It is one I am known for and have cooked for friends and family countless times. On the few occasions on the road with Howl that we get to have a nice home-cooked meal, this sort of dish (though it may vary to some degree) is something we all enjoy and need from time to time. It is packed full of nutrition and gives you a ton of energy— something we all need when facing the perils of tour. Plus it has a bunch of real vegetables!—something that gets pretty hard to come by on the road.

**SERVES 6 TO 8**

Two 14-ounce packages extra firm tofu
Vegetable oil
Soy sauce
1 large yam or sweet potato, peeled
2 large red onions
3 bell peppers (your choice of color)
1 large crown broccoli
One 15-ounce can baby corn, drained
Two 8-ounce cans sliced water chestnuts, drained
3 large garlic cloves
Sesame oil (optional)
2 large bunches kale (I prefer red leaf)
One 16-ounce package wide rice noodles
Two 14-ounce cans coconut milk
One 4-ounce can or jar red curry paste

Cut the tofu to desired size cubes or triangles. I recommend cutting each piece in half the thin way and then starting to cut diagonally corner to corner and across the middle of each side. Continue this trend for smaller triangles. Add to a hot frying pan with ¼-inch vegetable oil. When one side of the tofu begins to brown, add a few tablespoons of soy sauce. Brown on all sides and cook to desired texture.

Chop all of the vegetables to desired size pieces.

Add your chopped yam to a pot of boiling water. Boil until tender but not too soft (5 to 8 minutes). Drain.

In a large wok or skillet, fry onions and bell peppers in a little oil.

When onions start to become tender, add the broccoli, yam, baby corn, and water chestnuts and stir-fry.

In a separate wok or large skillet add finely diced garlic in vegetable oil (you could add a splash of sesame oil if desired).

When garlic begins to brown, add your chopped kale with about ⅓ cup of soy sauce and a little bit of water. Cook until the kale wilts, constantly mixing with the garlic and sauce.

In a large pot of boiling water, add the full package of rice noodles. Boil 6 to 8 minutes, until tender. Drain and set aside.

In your large wok with your vegetables, add the coconut milk. Add curry paste to desired spiciness (1 to 3 tablespoons). Mix vegetables with curry and coconut milk until the sauce begins to thicken.

Mix in your nicely browned tofu with the vegetables.

Serve the mixed vegetables and tofu in curry sauce on a plate over a bed of rice noodles. Serve your garlicky kale on the side.

# GRILLED PIZZA

## Tim "Ripper" Owens, *Judas Priest/Iced Earth/Yngwie Malmsteen*

**M**y wife Jeannie loves to cook, as do my kids, Timmy and Taylor, but they like to do it without our help. So that's how the pizza thing started. It's fun, and we love to make it and put it on the grill and hang as a family. But it is still a bit messy with two small children, who think they are chefs!

SERVES 4

### DOUGH

1¼ cups warm water (100 to 110°F)

2 packages dry yeast

1 tablespoon honey or Sugar in the Raw

3 tablespoons olive oil, plus extra for drizzling

4 cups all-purpose flour, plus extra for kneading

2 teaspoons kosher salt

Oil, for the bowl

Cornmeal

### SAVORY TOPPINGS (YOU CHOOSE YOUR FAVORITES.) I LIKE MINE HOT, HOT, HOT—FAMILY DOES NOT, LOL)

Fresh mozzarella, grated

Italian fontina, grated

Goat cheese, sliced

Green, red and/or yellow bell pepper, cored, seeded, and sliced

Prosciutto or ham, thinly sliced

Fresh spinach, cleaned

Plum tomatoes, sliced

Pork or turkey sausages, cooked and sliced

Pepperoni, sliced

1 bunch basil leaves, cleaned and dried

Roasted garlic cloves
Red pepper flakes

**SWEET TOPPINGS**
Peanut butter
Apples, cored and sliced
Caramel sauce
Cinnamon and sugar

For the dough, combine the water, yeast, honey, and olive oil in the bowl of an electric mixer fitted with a dough hook. Add 3 cups of the flour, then the salt, and mix. While mixing, add 1 cup more flour, or enough to make a soft dough. Knead the dough on low to medium speed for about 10 minutes, until smooth, sprinkling it with flour, if necessary, to prevent it from sticking to the bowl.

When the dough is ready, turn it out onto a floured board and knead by hand a dozen times. It should be smooth and elastic. Place the dough in a well-oiled bowl and turn it several times so that it's covered lightly with oil. Cover the bowl with a kitchen towel. Allow the dough to rest at room temperature for 30 minutes.

Divide the dough into six equal parts, and roll each one into a smooth ball. Place the balls on a baking sheet and cover them with a damp towel. Allow the dough to rest for 10 minutes. Use immediately, or refrigerate for up to 4 hours.

If you've chilled the dough, take it out of the refrigerator 30 minutes ahead to let it come to room temperature. Roll and stretch each ball into a rough 8-inch circle and place them all on baking sheets sprinkled with cornmeal.

Preheat the grill to 300°F. Place the pizzas directly onto the grill and cook on 1 side for 1 minute. Turn the pizzas over and brush with olive oil or garlic oil.

Top the pizzas with your favorite toppings. Drizzle each pizza with 1 tablespoon olive oil. Close the lid on your grill and cook for 5 minutes more, until the crust is crisp and the toppings are cooked.

# SOUTHERN KICKIN' CHICKEN AND BACON

## Cliff Rigano, *Dry Kill Logic*

**T**his recipe is best if all the ingredients are organic so you aren't chowing down on a bunch of chemicals.

SERVES 3 OR 4

3 shots tequila, in separate glasses

6 boneless, skinless chicken breast halves

1 pint grape tomatoes

12 fresh jalapeño chiles

2 large onions

1 cup grated cheddar cheese (about 4 ounces)

Salt

Black pepper

Diced garlic (fresh or bottled, NO garlic salt or powder/dried flakes)

Red pepper flakes

1 cup cheap tequila in a soup bowl

1 pound sliced bacon

One 20-ounce bottle Soy Vay Island Teriyaki Sauce (any teriyaki will do)

Before you start cooking, take a shot of tequila . . . ahhh, there you go.

Clean the chicken breasts and pound them breasts down as thin as possible with a meat hammer (not *your* meat hammer, *a* meat hammer) so that the breasts are as flat as possible (like pancakes, you know . . . you know you have seen pancake breasts before, I'm just sayin' . . . ).

Finely chop the tomatoes, jalapeños, and onions and combine in a bowl. Add the cheddar cheese. Season with salt, pepper, garlic, and red pepper flakes to taste. Place a good portion of the mixture in the flattened chicken breast and roll the chicken up like a burrito.

Dip the rolled-up chicken breast into the tequila and thoroughly wet the outside.

Take two pieces of bacon and wrap the rolled-up chicken. If you feel like the chicken isn't wrapping neatly, either remove some of the stuffing, or use a toothpick to keep the bacon and chicken wrapped together.

Clean your grill and get all the residual crap off it. Fire up your barbeque pit as hot as you can get it or heat a grill to 600°F. Let it preheat for 10 minutes.

Once the grill is hot like an Asian hooker, drop the wrapped up chicken on the grill and reduce the heat 30 percent. It's important to note that if you are worried about the bacon sticking to the grill, you can put down a piece of aluminum foil and cook the chicken on there. It might actually cook the bacon a bit more evenly, but whatever floats your boat.

Once the chicken begins to cook, take the second tequila shot. DEEEEEE-LISH.

It will take 10 to 15 minutes for the chicken to cook. Now is a good time to ingest some chemicals, especially the smokable kind . . . does an appetite good!

As the bacon begins to brown, make sure to turn the chicken over and cook the bacon evenly. (Watch for bacon fat flare-ups. I usually handle them by limiting the amount of time the grill top is down.)

Once the chicken breasts are 98 percent cooked, baste them with teriyaki sauce to taste. Once basted, turn the grill off and let them sit for 2 minutes to cool down.

Take the last tequila shot, put your chemicals away, take the chicken off the grill and EAT!

# SAUSAGE CURRY

## Blaze Bayley, *Iron Maiden/Wolfsbane*

An invigorating "after the pub" recipe developed by me and my mountain bike buddy, Mark. Now my brother and my father-in-law have both developed their own versions of my signature dish. My version is based on what was left in my fridge when we got back from the pub! A typical British night out would be a heavy drinking session from 8:30 PM to 11:00 PM followed by take-out or a meal in an Indian restaurant. We would have spent all our money on beer, and my house was closer than the ATM, so out of sheer necessity, sausage curry was born.

This dish is not a healthy option. If you don't break into a sweat and have a runny nose while eating it, you have to add an extra teaspoon of hot chili powder the next time you attempt to make it. This recipe does not conform to any normal cooking rules and should not be used as part of any diet for people with a weak bowel. It is an aggressive, almost masochistic dish, which is to be endured as much as it is enjoyed. That is why I think British men find it so invigorating.

**SERVES 4**

8 pints draught Guinness
1 tablespoon olive oil
1 medium onion
8 large top-quality pork sausages
2 whole bulbs (heads) garlic
2 teaspoons ground black pepper
1 teaspoon hot chili powder

One 10-ounce jar Vindaloo curry paste
1 bottle Chilean red wine
One 14.5-ounce can diced tomatoes
1 mug basmati rice
Juice of ½ lemon
1 teaspoon salt

Go to the pub. Drink the Guinness. Each person has to learn their own limits for alcohol. Only drink as much as you feel you can without impairing your ability to read large print or stagger for a half-mile. Also, if you can't hold a conversation about *Star Wars* or Black Sabbath, you have drunk too much. That's just a guide, okay? Walk the half-mile home, and think about your favorite spicy food.

Heat the olive oil over very low heat. (The perfect pan for this dish is a large, non-stick wok but any nonstick pan will do if you are desperate.)

Chop half the onion into very small pieces. Put the chopped onion into the wok and stir it a couple of times. Roughly chop the rest of the onion. Save a few pieces for garnish later, then add the roughly chopped onion to the wok and stir it in. The idea is to gently fry the onion on a low heat while you are getting everything else ready.

Cut the sausages into four pieces each and place in the wok with the onions. Turn up the heat slightly and occasionally stir the sausages and onion. Keep an eye on the wok and don't let anything burn. At this stage, everything should be nice and gentle like the first kiss to a baby coming home from the hospital.

Peel and thinly slice the garlic. Add to the wok and gently stir it in. Tips and hints for the preparation of garlic and onions are in my DVD, *Cooking on the Edge of Self-Destruction*, which comes out eventually—when I've made it.

Add the pepper and the chili powder, and stir them in. When the sausages are actually frying, add the curry paste and keep stirring while it heats up and starts to cook with the sausages.

When the skin on the sausages is brown, and the pieces seem to be cooked through, open the wine. Pour two large glasses for yourself and your friend. Put about half a cupful into the wok and get the whole thing sizzling and keep stirring. Be careful—at this point you have a wok that has hot fat and even hotter spices. If any of this spits and goes in your eyes, you will be in real pain and might need a trip to the emergency room. Take care because the embarrassment of saying to the lady in Admissions that you burned your eyes with hot fat while you were following a recipe by someone called Blaze Bayley is gonna be even more painful.

Add the tomatoes. Stir them in and keep all the ingredients simmering whilst stirring occasionally.

The rice: follow the instructions on the packet. A lot of rice comes with different cooking times. For the best results, follow the cooking time to the second. Add the lemon and the salt to the water before putting the rice in. When the rice is cooked, the sausage curry should be ready. Always let rice stand and drain for at least 1 minute before serving. Make sure the plates are warm but not too hot. The plates must not be cold.

Put some rice in the center of the plate and then put some of the sausage curry on top of it so you almost can't see the rice. Place the bits of onion you saved from earlier on top of the curry in the shape of a B.

Make sure you have some kitchen towels or tissues to wipe your brow as you enjoy the feeling of being burned to the point of agony knowing that you are doing this to yourself and not paying a chef in an Indian restaurant to do it to you.

Sip the red wine as you eat. Don't drink beer with spicy food. If you have a choice, choose a nice Chilean red wine. Preferably Casa el Diabolic. And stay away from water. Any bits of your tongue that have gone numb will come back to life and hurt you all over again.

If you follow my recipe, then I hope that you enjoy the result. The single most important ingredient is not listed. It is the friend called Mark. He really made the night that I invented sausage curry one that we would never forget. Whatever you have in your fridge or your bank account doesn't matter as much as the friends you share these moments with. Good luck with your cooking and the ingredients of your life.

# TARRAGON SALMON

## Bobby Blitz, *Overkill*

**A**nnette and I are year 'round BBQ junkies—sun/snow/wind/hurricane—we light the coals. And that's the key: coals. I've used a traditional Weber for the last twelve years and love it. It never burns, and it flavors meat and fish with that outdoor, summertime, fun flavor. Tarragon salmon is one of my faves based on the combination of ingredients that together make a spicy blend of sweet-meets-sting. Give it a whirl. "Fish up" with the KILL!

**SERVES 2**

2 tablespoons Dijon mustard
2½ tablespoons olive oil
1½ tablespoons brown sugar
2 tablespoons chopped fresh tarragon (or 2 teaspoons dried)
2 salmon steaks or 1 salmon fillet

Combine the mustard, oil, sugar, and tarragon. Spoon over the salmon (best when marinated overnight in the fridge.) Preheat the broiler or preheat the grill to 300°F.

Broil or grill 15 to 20 minutes, depending on thickness.

Fast, easy, and tasty. Just the way we like it!

# BEARDED CLAMS CASINO LINGUINE

## Dan Torelli, *Madina Lake*

It started back when we were in an apartment in L.A., making our first record in 2006. We would write and record all day in a small studio and then all come back "home" to an even smaller apartment at night and try to let out all of our frustrations and insecurities by hanging around the small kitchen island and talking, drinking, and cooking. Most of the time it was something along the lines of microwaveable mac and cheese or peanut butter and jelly sandwiches, but we decided one night to pull all our extra money together, go to the store, and then make as close to a real nice dinner as we could. As we were talking about our favorite flavors, someone mentioned clams casino and it sounded amazing to all of us. We definitely couldn't afford a few dozen clams and didn't know how we would cook them anyway, so we just bought all the flavors we could remember clams casino having and dumped it over some pasta and it worked out great! It was our first experience doing something like that as a band and it turned out to be pretty ridiculous. Now, not only does that dish taste good to us every time we've made it since, but it brings back some hilarious memories as well!

**SERVES 2**

Two 6.5-ounce cans chopped or minced clams
One 8-ounce bottle clam juice
Two 28-ounce cans diced tomatoes
1 garlic clove, chopped
1 small green bell pepper, chopped
½ white onion, chopped
Salt and pepper
Red pepper flakes (use as much or little as you want,
    depending on how spicy you like it)
Basil
Parsley

◆◆◆◆◆◆◆◆◆◆◆◆◆◆◆◆◆◆◆◆◆◆◆◆◆◆◆◆◆◆◆◆◆◆◆◆◆◆◆◆◆◆◆◆◆◆

8 to 10 Vicodin, crushed (optional, but recommended)

Fake bacon chips

1 pound linguine

Grated pecorino Romano cheese

Mix everything but the bacon chips, linguine, and cheese in a big pot and heat over medium heat for 45 minutes or so. Boil 1 pound linguine. When the linguine is almost done add the bacon chips to the sauce. Pour the sauce over the cooked linguine and top with Romano cheese.

# SEAFOOD LINGUINE

## CJ, *The Wildhearts*

First off, I never cook from recipes. I just make it up as I go along. I love coming up with new ideas and trying different ways to make classic dishes. My seafood linguine might make some Italians, or anyone who believes that you must follow authentic recipes, angry. So what, this is the way I do it and I like it!

When it comes to cooking, it's all about the taste and aroma. Who cares how you get there, as long as you enjoy yourself and your food puts a smile on someone's face? I'm a free spirit in the kitchen and with this recipe, as with all, you must adapt according to your taste. Enjoy!

SERVES 2

1 medium red onion

3 garlic cloves

¼ cup extra virgin olive oil

1 tablespoon butter

1 vegetable bouillon cube

One 14-ounce can chopped tomatoes

2 bay leaves

3 thyme sprigs

½ teaspoon cracked black pepper

A good pinch of sea salt

1 teaspoon Italian seasoning

A dash of balsamic vinegar

Red wine (optional)

Red pepper flakes (optional)

1 pound mussels, crayfish, cleaned squid, or shrimp (cooked or raw)

½ pound linguine

Sunglasses optional!

Roughly chop the onion and garlic, and blend in a food processor to a paste.

Pour the olive oil into a large pan and heat gently. Add the garlic and onion paste and fry gently for a couple of minutes. Stir occasionally and make sure it doesn't burn. Add the butter and the bouillon cube to the pan and stir well.

Puree half the tomatoes in a food processor and add this, plus the rest of the can, to the pan and heat gently (save the empty can for the next steps). Add the bay leaves, thyme, pepper, salt, and Italian seasoning to the pan.

Using the empty tomato can, fill with water, and add to the pan. Add a dash of balsamic vinegar at this point too (you may also want to add half a glass of good red wine and maybe some red pepper flakes if you like it a bit spicy).

Taste the sauce, but remember you will need to simmer it for 10 to 15 minutes, until it is of a thick consistency and the flavors are intensified. Add extra seasoning if required.

When you think the sauce is ready and you're happy with the flavors, add your seafood. If the seafood is precooked, just heat through gently. If it's raw, lightly poach in the tomato sauce until the mussel shells open (discard any that don't) or the crayfish, squid, or shrimp are just opaque all the way through.

Boil the linguine for approximately 10 minutes (cooking instructions may vary), then drain. Mix the pasta through the sauce and serve immediately with garlic bread, Parmesan, and black pepper to taste.

# BUSTED CHOPS

## John Ricco, *Warrior Soul*

**A**fter being on the road for months, it's nice to come home and throw something together that is not only easy to make but also tastes great. The thing I love about "Johnny Ricco's Busted Chops" is that it goes with any alcoholic beverage of choice.

**SERVES 3 OR 4**

6 pork chops

Lawry's Seasoned Salt (or similar seasoning)

4 russet (baking) potatoes, cubed

½ pound carrots, chopped

2 Spanish onions, chopped

One 12-ounce bottle Cardini's Italian Dressing (or similar)

Preheat the oven to 375°F.

Rinse your pork chops and place them in a glass or ceramic casserole. Sprinkle seasoned salt on the chops. Spread the potatoes, carrots, and onions all around and on top (the way I like my girls) of the pork chops. Cover everything with the dressing. Cover with foil and place in the oven for 1½ to 2 hours. Leave uncovered the last half-hour.

Guaranteed to satisfy! Enjoy!

# SHRIMP AND PASTA WITH BROCCOLI

## Diamond Dave Ardolina, *Moth Eater*

**T**his is my all-time favorite dish! After a long day of truckin' or rockin' out with Moth Eater, it's the best. In a world where many people are cutting carbs, I say, "The hell with that!" Carbs, carbs, I love carbs! Everyone should have some shrimp and pasta every night. You'll be twenty pounds overweight like myself in no time. I guarantee it. Most importantly, have your wife or your girlfriend cook this while she's naked for the best possible flavoring. It's delicious!!!

Enjoy . . .

**SERVES 2 TO 4**

1 pound frozen cooked peeled shrimp (size 31–40)
Two 10-ounce packages frozen broccoli spears
1 tablespoon chopped garlic
1 tablespoon dried parsley flakes
½ teaspoon sea salt
½ teaspoon ground black pepper
¼ cup olive oil
3 tablespoons butter
¼ cup dry white wine
1 pound linguine, cooked

Thaw the shrimp. Remove the tail shells if they're on. Thaw the broccoli spears in the microwave until almost completely thawed, but still cold. Set aside for later use.

Using a frying pan, sauté the garlic, parsley, salt, and pepper in the olive oil and butter until the garlic sizzles. Add broccoli and white wine and cook for 7 to 10 minutes over medium-low heat. Once broccoli is fully cooked (bright green), add the shrimp and let it cook for another 7 to 10 minutes, stirring frequently. Serve over linguine and enjoy!

‑

# THE REJAS FROM TEJAS BBQ FROM HELL

## Rex, *Down/Pantera*

This is one of my favorites because everyone that I make it for freaks out. If it starts to burn a little on top, don't worry—just turn the flame down or open the grill. It will make your tongue slap the back of your brain. Also try halved peaches splashed with balsamic vinegar on the grill.

SERVES 2 TO 4

2 to 3 pounds beef tenderloin, in one piece
Garlic salt
Pepper
Lemon pepper
Seasoned salt
Red pepper flakes
Two 16-ounce bottles Newman's Own Caesar Dressing

Turn on your gas grill (preferably four-burner) to 250°F.

Rub meat with the dry seasonings, to taste—let her have it!!! Pour 1 bottle of the dressing all over it. Repeat rub—again let her have it!!! Repeat dressing. Repeat rub, so it makes a glaze. Marinate for 20 minutes.

Place the meat on the grill. Turn off the burners directly under the meat so it cooks over indirect heat. Let cook for 2 to 3 hours, until your meat thermometer reaches 145°F.

Take off immediately and cover with foil. It will keep cooking off the grill. That's it. Bon appétit, or as they say in Tejas . . . Get after it!!!

# BARD SCRAMBLE

## Otep

This is how you should start every day. This breakfast will get you going.

Onion
Butter
Spices (cayenne, red pepper flakes,
   Mediterranean sea salt, black
   pepper, paprika, rosemary)
4 eggs
Milk (dairy or soy)

Frank's Red Hot Sauce
Your favorite fine Irish whiskey or
   Scotch (Johnnie Walker Black,
   Bushmills, Glenlivet, etc.)
4-cheese mix (swiss, mozzarella,
   asadero, Monterey Jack)

Prepare your onions, diced, sliced, or minced. Heat a skillet with butter and cook until melted. Add the onions. Sprinkle with your desired hot spices. Cook the onions slowly so as not to burn.

Mix 3 of the eggs with a dash of milk, a splash of Frank's Red Hot Sauce, some crushed rosemary, and a half-cap of your favorite whiskey or Scotch. Pour the mixture into the pan over the onions. Stir mixture gently, pulling the edges away from the pan as it solidifies.

Sprinkle additional spices over the eggs as they cook, including a bit of Mediterranean sea salt and black pepper.

Keep turning eggs over and over to get a nice fluffy scramble. When the eggs are almost cooked, add 1 additional egg over entire pan. Stir the new egg into the cooked ones so that it adds to the texture, color, and flavor.

Once the eggs are done, remove from heat, place them on a plate, and sprinkle your favorite cheeses over steaming eggs, mixing the cheese into them so it gets a nice melt.

Bon appétit!

# SEARED TUNA WITH WASABI-BUTTER SAUCE

## Ryan Martinie, *Mudvayne*

Prep Time: approx 5 minutes

SERVES 6

- 2 tablespoons white wine vinegar
- 1¼ cups white wine
- ¼ cup minced shallots
- 1 tablespoon wasabi paste, or to taste
- 1 tablespoon soy sauce
- 16 tablespoons (2 sticks) unsalted butter, cubed
- Six 6-ounce fresh tuna steaks, 1-inch thick
- 1 tablespoon olive oil, or as needed
- Salt and black pepper

Combine the vinegar, wine, and shallots in a small saucepan over medium heat. Simmer until the liquid is reduced to about 2 tablespoons. Strain out the shallot and discard, return liquid to pan. Stir the wasabi and soy sauce into the reduction. Over low heat, gradually whisk the butter one cube at a time, allowing the mixture to emulsify. Be careful not to let the mixture boil. When all of the butter has been incorporated, remove from heat. Pour into a small bowl and set aside.

Heat a large skillet over medium-high heat. Brush the tuna steaks with olive oil and season with salt and pepper. Place in the hot skillet and sear from 3 to 5 minutes on each side. Be careful not to overcook; this fish should be served still a little pink in the center. Serve with the sauce.

# ORANGE TEQUILA SHRIMP

## Joey Belladonna, *Anthrax*

This specific dish is my favorite because I love shrimp and was quite fond of tequila back in the day. This dish came about when my wife and I were cooking one day in the kitchen and took some ideas and ran with it. When you combine tequila and oranges while cooking, the end result is always a fiery bang!

We serve it with Margarita mixes mixed with club soda in place of tequila for the nondrinkers. Chips and fresh salsa as a small starter, and my favorite, vanilla ice cream, for dessert. Try to find the chipotle chiles. They add terrific flavor.

**SERVES 4**

6 tablespoons (¾ stick) unsalted butter
2 tablespoons finely chopped white onion
2 garlic cloves, minced
16 large shrimp, peeled and deveined
½ to 1 teaspoon finely chopped chipotle chile in adobo or
    1 serrano chile, finely chopped
¼ teaspoon orange oil
¼ cup tequila reposado
2 to 2½ tablespoons minced fresh cilantro
Sea salt

In a sauté pan over medium heat, melt the butter. Add the onion and sauté until it is translucent, 3 to 4 minutes. Add the garlic and shrimp and cook, stirring frequently, until the shrimp turn pink and begin to curl, 4 to 5 minutes. Be careful not to overcook the shrimp.

Add the chiles and orange oil. Stir to mix. Pour the tequila over the shrimp, ignite carefully with a long match, and let the flames burn out. Add the minced cilantro, season with sea salt, and serve.

# ITALIAN SPAGHETTI SAUCE AND MEATBALLS

## Zakk Wylde, *Black Label Society/Ozzy Osbourne*

**H**anded down generation to generation . . . homemade. Make your pasta al dente, and enjoy.

FEEDS THE WHOLE FAMILY

### SAUCE

⅛ teaspoon olive oil (just enough to spread on bottom of large skillet)

2 or 3 garlic cloves, minced

2 pounds pork meat on bones*

1 package sweet or hot Italian sausage (I use hot)

Four 28-ounce cans Italian tomatoes, crushed or peeled (any brand)

1 teaspoon chopped fresh basil

1 cup grated Italian cheese (Locatelli, Parmesan, or Romano—I prefer Locatelli)

1 hard-boiled egg, unpeeled

Meatballs (recipe follows)

Salt

In a large skillet, heat the olive oil and garlic on low heat. Add the pork. Brown the meat on each side.

Brown sausage on all sides in a separate skillet.

While meat is browning, combine 1 can of the tomatoes in a blender with ¼ teaspoon of the basil, ¼ cup of the grated cheese, and 2 tablespoons cold water. Blend until pureed. Repeat for each can of tomatoes. Pour pureed tomatoes into a large stockpot and begin to cook sauce on a low flame.

When the meats are browned, add to the tomatoes. Scrape most of the fat drippings out of the two skillets and add ½ cup water to each pan to make a gravy (it should sizzle when you add the water), then add it to the sauce. Add the unpeeled hard-boiled egg, just to remove acidity from sauce; discard after sauce is complete. Cook the sauce on low heat for approximately 3 hours, or less if it thickens faster. Stir every so often so the tomatoes do not stick to the bottom of the pot. When the sauce is halfway done, add your meatballs.

You can use salt to taste after the sauce is made—taste first as grated cheese can be salty.

*I use 3 large center-cut pork chops with some fat on, or you can use baby pork spare ribs—about 6 or 7, or you can ask your butcher for pork bones with some meat on.

## MEATBALLS

2½ pounds ground beef (do not use sirloin)

¼ pound ground pork

¼ pound ground veal

2 garlic cloves

¼ teaspoon chopped fresh basil

¼ cup whole or low-fat milk

3 large eggs

1 cup dry bread crumbs

1 slice stale white bread, torn into several pieces

¼ cup grated cheese (again, your preference: Locatelli, Parmesan, or Romano)

Olive oil

In a large bowl, mix together the ground meats, using your hands.

In a blender, mix the garlic, basil, milk, and eggs until liquid. Fold in the bread crumbs, stale bread, and grated cheese. Pour into the bowl with the ground meat. Again using your hands, make sure meat is blended with the mixture, and form your meatballs.

Brown the meatballs in a small amount of olive oil. Brown only the top and bottom and add to sauce when sauce is half cooked.

# WELFARE WEDGES

## Jason Decay, *Cauldron*

I've been making these a lot lately 'cause they're cheap. When everyone else is showing up to the barbeque with their fancy veggie kebob steaks and gourmet burger meat, I'm rockin' a ten-pound bag of potatoes and a 6 of Bavarian talls. . . .

Clean potatoes and cut into wedges. Put them on a piece of aluminum foil with some olive oil (make sure oil gets between the wedges and the foil).

Mince 1 clove of garlic per potato or shake on some garlic powder. Sprinkle the potatoes with rosemary. Douse with hot sauce. Splash with beer.

Fold the foil over to cover potatoes and throw them on your double bunk-b-que on high heat for 10 to 15 minutes per side.

If you're scared of barbeques in the winter, you can always do this in the oven on high heat for about the same time. Enjoy!

# KRAKATOA SURPRISE

## Lemmy, *Motörhead*

Note from the Editor: In theory, this is an awesome recipe, but prepare at your own risk.

- ¼ pound flour
- ½ pound chocolate syrup
- ¼ pound refried beans
- ½ pound curry powder
- 1 bottle strawberry syrup
- ¼ bottle brandy

Mix flour, syrup, beans, and curry powder into a model of Krakatoa Island. Pour strawberry syrup over it to simulate lava. Pour brandy over all. Strike a match. Eat while still burning.

SURPRISE!

# THE STUFFING WITHIN

## Matthew Bachand, *Shadows Fall*

This is a twist on something I tried while we were on tour in Greece. I loved it so much, as soon as I got home I tried to recreate it with a few alterations. It's great for all you veggies out there, too. You will need a 6-pack of nice, cheap beer (Pabst, Busch, etc.) before you begin. BOTTOMS UP!!!

**SERVES 2 TO 4**

4 large, firm tomatoes

1 small onion, diced

1 small shallot, chopped

1 garlic clove, minced

3 tablespoons olive oil

6 cans cheap beer

1½ cups chopped, cooked spinach

¼ cup dry bread crumbs

1½ cups cooked white rice

1 egg

¼ cup crumbled feta cheese

1 teaspoon salt

1 teaspoon ground pepper

2 teaspoons dried dill weed

2 teaspoons dried basil

1 tablespoon hot sauce (optional)

¼ cup shredded mozzarella cheese

Preheat the oven to 375°F.

Cut tomatoes in half crosswise and scoop out the innards. Set the tomato halves aside. Drain the water from the innards and chop the innards well.

In a saucepan, sauté the onion, shallot, and garlic in 1 tablespoon of the olive oil.

Drink one beer.

In a large bowl, combine the cooked onions and garlic with the spinach, bread crumbs, rice, egg, feta cheese, salt, pepper, dill, basil, hot sauce (if using), and to-mato innards. Mix well.

Drink a second beer.

Stuff the tomatoes with the mixture. Place in a casserole. Pour the remaining 2 tablespoons of olive oil evenly over the stuffed tomatoes.

Bake for 15 to 20 minutes, until the stuffing begins to firm up on top.

Drink a third beer while you wait.

Sprinkle the mozzarella on top of the tomatoes and place back in the oven until cheese is melted.

Enjoy the remaining three beers with your meal.

◆◆◆◆◆◆◆◆◆◆◆◆◆◆◆◆◆◆◆◆◆◆◆◆◆◆◆◆◆◆◆◆◆◆◆◆◆◆◆◆◆◆◆◆◆◆◆◆◆◆

# LIPS'S PIZZA FRIES

## Steve "Lips" Kudlow, *Anvil*

This is one of my recipes that is great to make on the road or while you are just relaxing at home.

**SERVES 2 TO 4**

1 pound lean ground beef
One 24-ounce can Unico pasta sauce (or your favorite brand)
One 2-pound bag McCain frozen french fries (ditto)
8 ounces shredded mozzarella cheese

Preheat the oven to 425°F.

Brown the meat in a skillet and drain the fat away.

Pour the pasta sauce into a large saucepan. Add the browned meat, and bring sauce to a boil.

Once the oven is heated up, spread the fries onto a cookie sheet and cook for 20 minutes until golden brown.

Let the sauce slowly simmer until it thickens up. When the fries are ready, take out of the oven and pour sauce over the fries. Sprinkle shredded mozzarella on top. Return to oven for about 5 minutes, until cheese is melted.

Remove and dish onto plates to serve.

# STUFFED LOBSTER ZAMPELLA

## Joey Zampella, *Life of Agony*

This is my own personal specialty dish that I've created that always seems to deliver a knockout punch to any lobster lover.

**SERVES 1 OR 2**

Purchase your 1¾-pound live lobsters no more than a couple of hours before cooking. Refrigerate them and allow some air to get into the bag. You don't want to suffocate the little guys. You need them alive, or they're no good!

## STEP ONE-"The Broth"

To begin, fill a large 20 to 24–quart pot two-thirds of the way up with water. Add ½ cup virgin olive oil, 1 cup lemon juice, 6 chunks of fresh garlic (sliced in half), ¼ cup salt, and a palmful of black pepper, then cover the pot and bring to a boil. Easy enough.

## STEP TWO-"The Goods"

Since that water is going to take some time to boil, we jump straight into the stuffing. Now, I'm writing this recipe for two, so any more lobsters you add, just add an equal amount of ingredients. You will need ½ pound fresh shrimp (peeled and cleaned), ½ pound fresh scallops, ½ pound artificial crab, 2 sleeves of Ritz crackers (half a 16-ounce box), and 1 egg.

Soak your fish (shrimp, scallops, and crab) for 10 minutes in cold water and a bit of salt. Drain then dice it all into small pieces. In a large sauté pan, melt a generous chunk of butter over medium-to-high heat. Throw the fish into the pan and add a bit of chopped garlic for extra flavor. Stir occasionally and allow fish to cook thoroughly while making its own juice in the pan. When it's finished take it off the heat and set it aside.

In a large bowl, crush two sleeves of crackers, but not too finely. You want them a bit chunky. Add the fish with its juice to the crackers and drop that egg in there (of course, without the shell). Throw in a bit of pepper, then mix with a big spoon until it starts to look like stuffing! Add more crackers if needed, then set that aside. Step two is done!!

## STEP THREE-"The Execution"

This is the step that is a bit uncomfortable for some people. If such is the case with you, call the craziest person in your house into the kitchen and have them do it, because you're about to murder the lobsters!! I have a funny, quick true story to add here . . . I made this stuffed lobster dish for Kirk Hammett and his wife at their house once. Kirk refused to let me throw the lobsters in the boiling water while they were awake! He swore to me that he heard there was a way to put them to sleep. I didn't believe him, so he searched the Web for "how to hypnotize a lobster," and he was right!! There it was!!! All you have to do is lay them on their backs and in a minute or two they fall asleep!! So guess what I'll have you do in honor of Kirk. Take a minute to put the babies to sleep . . . THEN CHUCK THEM IN THE BOIL-ING WATER LIKE THE SAVAGE BEAST THAT YOU ARE!!!!! Oh, I'm sorry, didn't mean to scream.

Cook them together for 12 to 13 minutes. *Do not* empty the broth after boiling them. You will need it again!

## STEP FOUR-"The Glory"

So now that the lobsters are cooked and the stuffing is waiting, we have the celebratory meeting of two wonderfully tasting counterparts. First, preheat your oven to 400°F.

Now we need to split the lobsters, one at a time. Place them on their backs on a cutting board over your sink. Take a large, sharp butcher knife and carefully split the entire body and tail down the center (this will be the side you stuff). Empty out all the internal crap, using a spoon and running warm water. Then take a set of tongs and redip each lobster in your broth just to coat them with more flavor.

Place them on a large baking pan. Open the bodies a bit more by taking your hands and cracking them open wider. From here you just want to cram as much of that stuffing in and on top of them as you can. Drizzle a little oil across the top, put the pan in the oven, and let bake for 15 to 20 minutes, no cover. When that's done, flash it under your broiler for a couple of minutes to brown the top of the stuffing and . . . WELCOME TO HEAVEN! GET CRACKING!!!

This meal is best served with a side of sautéed or creamed spinach, melted butter for dipping, and some lemon wedges. Thank you, and please don't sue me if your guests die of overstimulation.

# DRUNKEN BATTERED CHICKEN

### Ernie C, *Body Count*

**D**runken chicken is a meal I've made many times over the years. The first job I ever had in my life was KFC. When I cook fried chicken for my friends, I add vodka just to make it a little more spicy and a little more rock 'n' roll. It's great fun. Make some mashed potatoes, gravy, collard greens, macaroni and cheese, and some grape Kool-Aid. That'll finish off the meal, and you'll have a great dinner or party. Enjoy!

**FEEDS 4 TO 6 HUNGRY PEOPLE**

8 pieces chicken (thighs, drumsticks, whatever you like)
1½ cups whole milk
2 large eggs
2 ounces vodka (your favorite)
2 cups flour
½ teaspoon salt
¼ teaspoon black pepper
1 brown paper bag
1 tablespoon bacon grease
canola oil

Pour 2 inches of oil into a deep cast iron skillet.

In a large bowl, whisk together the eggs, milk, and vodka. Place the chicken into the bowl. Turn to coat and refrigerate for a minimum of 20 minutes.

Place flour, salt, and pepper in the brown paper bag and shake to mix.

Remove chicken pieces from bowl and place into the brown paper bag with the seasonings and shake to coat the chicken.

Heat the oil and bacon grease in the iron skillet to 375°F.

Once the oil is ready, place the chicken pieces carefully into the hot oil. Fry the chicken, turning only once, until the chicken is thoroughly cooked, about 20 minutes, and remove from pan.

# DRUNK TOURING BAND MUSH

## Erik Larson, *Alabama Thunderpussy*

**W**ell, I don't really have a recipe, per se, but here's something I like to make. Can be made vegan!

### FEEDS SEVEN OR EIGHT DRUNK BAND AND CREW MEMBERS

4 to 6 Yukon gold potatoes

5 or 6 baby bella mushrooms

½ red onion

3 large garlic cloves

1 tablespoon butter or margarine

2 good-size jalapeño chiles (substitute cayenne peppers or Thai chiles
    depending on tolerance for pain and degree of inebriation)

Basil (6 fresh leaves is best, but prepared shake bottle will work, too)

Vegetable oil

8 ounces sharp white cheddar cheese

First and foremost, the kitchen must be free and clear of all bullshit. This includes nu-metal, rap-core music, and fashion. If any hip-hop or rap is audible within 100 yards of the cooking process, the food will spoil. You need good metal or crust punk to make this dish work. So pick a record, and turn it up loud! (I've found the first Tragedy record to be ideal chopping vegetable music.)

Anyhow, wash the potatoes and all the vegetables under clean running water and set aside.

Fill a large pot, big enough for Rosie O'Donnell's severed head, with water and place on back burner on high. While the water is heating up, chop the potatoes into small pieces, about the size of the bottom of a 1-ounce shot glass, placing the pieces in the pot as you chop. Periodically stir the pot of potatoes as you bring them to a boil.

◆◆◆◆◆◆◆◆◆◆◆◆◆◆◆◆◆◆◆◆◆◆◆◆◆◆◆◆◆◆◆◆◆◆◆◆◆◆◆◆◆◆◆◆◆◆◆◆

Once all the potatoes are in the pot, cut the mushrooms into little pieces (size depends on preference, I like about the size of a quarter). Do the same for the onion and garlic (chopping to preference—I usually dice these so they're the size of a pinky nail or smaller).

Melt the butter in a small iron skillet and cook the mushrooms, onion, and garlic on low heat. Be sure to stir that shit up every now and then so it doesn't burn.

Meanwhile, chop the chiles into small pieces. Be sure to save all the seeds with the pepper sections. DO NOT DISPOSE OF THE SEEDS; ONLY LIGHTWEIGHTS DISPOSE OF THEIR SEEDS. If you have acquired fresh basil leaves, chop them into tiny pieces; if not, move on. Pour enough oil into the bottom of a large skillet to coat just the surface and place on a medium heat, adding the hot peppers and their seeds.

At this point, check the potatoes. They should be soft but still retaining shape, with a faded whitish color. If they are, dump those suckers into the colander and let them drain. Once drained, put them into the large skillet with the hot peppers and add the basil (if using a shaker of basil, lightly coat the surface of the potatoes so they look kinda dirty). Stir the contents of the large skillet until the potatoes have lost shape and have become a mush-like substance. Add the mushrooms, onion, and garlic to the mix and continue cooking over medium heat, stirring frequently until it starts to brown (add oil as needed so as not to burn the bottom of the skillet or potatoes).

Once the mix seems sufficiently cooked through and brown, turn off stove and remove from heat. Grate cheese over the mix as desired. Cover to let the cheese melt. Serve with ketchup or hot sauce as needed. Pass out on the floor full. Enjoy!

# JIBARITO

## Gino, *Thick as Blood*

I'm Gino from Thick as Blood, and being a Latino, it's only appropriate for me to choose a Latin dish. I chose the Jibarito, a Puerto Rican sandwich. I chose it because it's amazing! It's quick to make and very filling. You can eat it for lunch with some fries and be satisfied for days. Ha-ha. I found out about it while I was visiting a friend in Chicago and have craved it ever since.

**SERVES 1**

- 2 cups vegetable oil for frying
- 1 green plantain, peeled and halved lengthwise
- 2 tablespoons vegetable oil
- 1 clove garlic, minced
- 4 ounces beef skirt steak, cut into thin strips
- ¼ medium yellow onion, thinly sliced
- 1 pinch cumin
- 1 pinch dried oregano
- 1 tablespoon mayonnaise
- 2 slices tomato
- 3 leaves iceberg lettuce, chopped or shredded

Heat two cups vegetable oil in a large, deep skillet or deep fryer to 350°F. Place plantain halves in the oil and cook for 1 to 2 minutes, until they float. Remove from oil and drain on paper towels.

Sandwich the plantain halves between two cutting boards. Press to flatten. Place the flattened plantains back in the oil and cook for 2 to 3 minutes, until golden brown. Drain on paper towels.

Heat 2 tablespoons of oil in a large skillet. Add the garlic, skirt steak, onion, cumin, and oregano. Cook, stirring frequently, until steak is cooked through.

To serve, spread mayonnaise on one of the plantain slices. Top with the steak and onion mixture, lettuce, and tomato. Place the other plantain half on top to form a sandwich. Cut in half and serve!

There you have it—a Jibarito from 47 Ave and Thick as Blood! Enjoy!

# CLAM SPAGHETTI

## Eric Peterson, *Testament/Dragonlord*

I love this recipe, first of all because I love pasta. Secondly, this tastes like restaurant food because it is nice and spicy, and I have been told that it is even better than restaurant food. My kids love it, too. Don't be scared to spice it up!!!

SERVES 4

1 large onion, chopped
2 teaspoons dried oregano
2 teaspoons dried basil
1 teaspoon cayenne pepper
5 or 6 garlic cloves, chopped fine
½ cup olive oil
Four 6.5-ounce cans minced clams
1 cup white wine
1 pound spaghetti or linguine
1 cup grated Parmesan cheese
½ cup chopped fresh parsley

Sauté the onion, oregano, basil, cayenne, and garlic in the olive oil. Add the juice from the clams and simmer for ½ hour.

Add the clams and white wine and simmer for 20 to 30 minutes more.

Meanwhile, cook the pasta according to package directions. Drain, return to the pasta pot and toss with the clam sauce. Add the Parmesan cheese and chopped parsley and toss again.

Enjoy with a nice cold chardonnay!

# THE ROCK 'N' ROLL SANDWICH

## Bruce Kulik, *KISS/Union*

An easy sandwich in the home or on the bus if you have a toaster oven.

**Sliced turkey or ham any style**
**Swiss cheese or substitute with provolone, American, etc.**
**Mustard (hot or mild)**
**Butter or margarine**
**Some mayo if you dare**
**Fresh hothouse tomatoes, as they are the juiciest**
**English muffins or a variation of**

Okay, here we go. . . .

Slice the muffins, toast lightly. Add mustard and/or butter or mayo etc., lay out pieces of cheese first, then add turkey or ham so they will fit nicely on the two sides of the muffin. Add sliced tomato. Place back in the toaster oven for a second heating. Yummy sandwich like the new chains make.

Variation: You can make an easy pizza this way. Spread on some good tomato sauce from the jar, add mozzarella cheese, add more sauce etc. Toast the same way. YEAH! For you hot freaks add your favorite salsa, etc.

ENJOY! Makes very quickly and with some chips, etc., is a good lunch. All the best.

# SASQUATCH SUNDAY GRAVY

## Keith Gibbs, *Sasquatch*

Sunday gravy is the ultimate Italian comfort food. When I was younger, Sunday was the day for the big family meal. My mom would start cooking the gravy early in the morning and simmer it all day long, filling the house with its wonderful smell. Throughout the day my younger brother and I would sneak into the kitchen and taste the gravy, hoping our mom wouldn't catch us. We just couldn't wait for dinner. Usually around five o'clock the gravy would finally be served with whichever pasta my mom felt like making that day, and it never disappointed.

**SERVES 4**

1 bottle (750 ml) Burgundy wine
½ pound Italian sausage
½ pound skinless, boneless chicken
    (whichever parts you like)
Fresh garlic
1 onion
Fresh parsley
Fresh oregano

Fresh basil
Olive oil
One 6-ounce can tomato paste
One 15-ounce can crushed tomatoes
One 14.5-ounce can diced tomatoes
Salt and pepper
Sugar

First thing you do is pour yourself a glass of the Burgundy and take a sip. All good gravy starts this way.

Take the casing off the sausage and chop into bite-size chunks. Prep the chicken with a nice rinse under the faucet and cut into chunks. Set aside.

Next, finely chop the garlic, onion, parsley, oregano, and basil. Get out a large stock-pot and turn the stovetop to medium-high heat. Pour some olive oil in the pan when it heats up, then add the onion and cook until it's almost transparent. Then add the garlic (do not brown). When the garlic starts to look a little bit transparent, add the tomato paste, stir, and fry all three ingredients together for about a minute.

Again, be careful not to brown.

Add the crushed and diced tomatoes, oregano to taste, basil (to taste), and parsley for color. Fill the empty tomato paste can with water and add that also. Next add the wine, I like to add at least three glugs (the sound the wine makes coming out of the bottle), or about a cup, cup and a half.

Next add salt, pepper, and sugar (to kill the acidity) to taste. Add the chicken and sausage and let the gravy simmer for 3 hours. Stir occasionally as it cooks, so that it doesn't burn or stick to the bottom of the pot.

Pour another glass of vino and add your favorite pasta!

◆◆◆◆◆◆◆◆◆◆◆◆◆◆◆◆◆◆◆◆◆◆◆◆◆◆◆◆◆◆◆◆◆◆◆◆◆◆◆◆◆◆◆◆◆◆◆◆◆

# SPICY SHRIMP AND SWEET CHERRY TOMATOES

## Scott Ian, *Anthrax*

I love this recipe because it's so damn easy to make, and it tastes so good!

**SERVES 4**

1 cup extra virgin olive oil

1 small onion, chopped fine

5 garlic cloves, chopped fine

4 dry pints small sweet cherry or grape tomatoes

Kosher salt

Freshly ground black pepper

½ to 1 teaspoon red pepper flakes

2 pounds rigatoni pasta

1 cup white wine

24 extra large shrimp, peeled, deveined, tails removed

Set a large pot of salted water to boil. Set a timer for 20 minutes.

Heat the oil in a large saucepan over high heat. When the oil is hot but not smoking, lower heat, add the onion, and cook until clear (do not brown). Add the garlic and cook until softened (once again, do not brown), usually 2 minutes tops.

To the saucepan, add the tomatoes, 6 pinches of kosher salt, 10 to 12 turns of a black pepper grinder, and red pepper flakes (amount depends on how hot you like it). Sauté the tomatoes until they start to pop, then cover the pan. Keep cooking over low-medium heat, stirring every 2 minutes.

When the pasta water comes to a boil, set a timer for 11 minutes and add the rigatoni to the boiling water. Eleven minutes is usually the perfect amount of time for your pasta to be done al dente. Don't overcook your pasta.

When there's 8 minutes left on the timer, add the wine to the saucepan (only use a wine that is good enough to drink).

When there's 6 minutes left, add the shrimp to the pan.

When your timer goes off, turn off the heat and let the sauce sit in the covered pan for 5 minutes while you drain your pasta. Plate, serve and enjoy!

# PROGRESSIVE METAL CHILI

## Kelly Shaefer, *Atheist*

This is my ode to the Cincinnati chili I grew up with. It's a variation that has a bit more flavor than the famous Cincy Chili, and it's far hotter (if you like). If you do it right, you should be able to cut the chili like a pie. Remember to cover the chili and pasta on your plate with lots of cheese (shredded) to get the pie effect. I cooked this for the Skid Row boys one time, and they loved it. It's my favorite as well! Enjoy!

**FEEDS THE WHOLE HOUSE**

One 8-ounce jar or can mushrooms, drained
½ onion, chopped
4 garlic cloves, finely diced
2 tablespoons olive oil
2 pounds ground beef
1 28-ounce can peeled tomatoes
1 28-ounce can tomatoes puree
1 jalapeño chile, minced (optional)
½ tablespoon ground cinnamon
Salt
4 or 5 tablespoons chili powder
One 14-ounce can beans, drained (optional)
8 ounces or more pasta, cooked
12 ounces shredded mild cheddar cheese

Sauté the metal mushrooms, onion, and garlic in the olive oil until browned. Add the ground beef, cook until slightly browned, then drain.

In a stockpot, get your chili sauce brewing by taking the peeled tomatoes and puree and putting them on medium to high heat until boiling. Then smash them until they liquefy.

Add the beef-mushroom mixture and jalepeño (if you want it hot) and mix together. Add your cinnamon and salt it up good (to taste).

Now the important part: you must use 4 to 5 tablespoons of chili powder, until the chili is dark in color. You can add beans if you like (I don't, personally).

Cook on medium heat for about 15 minutes, add pasta, and sprinkle heavily with cheese until the chili is completely covered.

Serve with red wine, beer, or my favorite, Mountain Dew! Enjoy!!!

P.S. This is a hangover cure as well! BEEEELCH!!!

# GARBAGE PLATE

## Acey Slade, *Dope/Murderdolls*

As a touring musician, you find yourself a citizen of the world, not calling any one place home. Home is where you hang your six-string. When I go on tour I try to hang out with as many people as I can and to take in something local so that I feel more at home in different places. One way of accomplishing this is by going out to a strip bar. But sometimes they are closed because of stupid blue laws. So instead I'll try to get some food after a show. If you are really lucky, you can find a strip bar that is open late and get a stripper to buy you dinner.

Anyway, I might be a scrawny, pale guy, but let me tell you, I love food. Pittsburgh has Pirami Bros. Chicago has Giordano's Pizza. Glasgow has deep-fried Mars bars. Tokyo has amazing Kobe beef. I basically know my way around the world by food. But the last place you would expect to find one of the best American dishes ever is in Rochester, New York. It's called the Garbage Plate, and the only place to get one is at a restaurant called Nick Tahou's.

So what is a Garbage Plate?

You get your choice of three materials. First is your "foundation." This is normally a meat: hot dog, hamburger, steak, fish patty, sausage. Second is your starch: French fries, home fries, etc. Third is your choice of baked beans, macaroni salad, coleslaw, you get the idea. You pick from these categories, and they are all thrown together on a plate so that they are piled on top of each other in a very disorganized fashion. Then add onions, mustard, and—this is key—the Special Hot Sauce!

This is the best food in the world at two-thirty in the morning. The more you mix it, and the colder it gets, the better. Road food doesn't get any better, and I would take this over a strip bar any day. I think.

If you work at Nick's, and I screwed anything up, please forgive me.

This is my attempt at a Cheeseburger Garbage Plate.

**FEEDS THE WHOLE BAND**

**SPECIAL HOT SAUCE**

1 medium onion, chopped

1 garlic clove, minced

1 tablespoon oil

1 pound triple-ground beef

1 cup water

One 6-ounce can tomato paste

½ tablespoon brown sugar (optional)

1 teaspoon ground black pepper

¾ tablespoon cayenne pepper

1 teaspoon chili powder

1½ teaspoons paprika

½ teaspoon ground cumin

½ teaspoon ground allspice

¼ teaspoon ground cinnamon

½ teaspoon ground cloves

Salt

**PLATE**

8 frozen beef patties

4 cups frozen hash browns

8 slices white American cheese

4 cups cold baked beans or 4 cups
  macaroni salad

Mustard

1 medium onion, diced

2 loaves of fresh Italian bread

40 salted butter pats, unwrapped

## Step 1 - Preparing the Special Hot Sauce

In a large frying pan, fry the onions and garlic in the oil. Add the meat, stirring constantly with a fork to keep its texture fine. Once the meat has browned, add the water and tomato paste. Simmer for 10 minutes. Add the sugar, spices, and salt to taste. Simmer for 30 minutes, adding water, if necessary, to keep it moist but not soupy.

## Step 2 - Preparing the Plate

You can substitute any of the other "foundation" items in place of the cheeseburger. These items are hamburger, beef hot dogs, steak (very popular), egg (I don't know about that), veggies (kind of defeats the purpose), or fish.

Take the beef patties straight out of the freezer and lightly sear on super hot griddle. Do the same with hash browns. Melt 1 slice of cheese on each beef patty. Add the griddle scrapings to the sauce.

Place a cup of baked beans or a cup of macaroni salad, and 1 cup of hash browns on a restaurant-style paper plate. Place 2 beef patties on top of the heap in the center. Spread mustard and diced onions over the beef patties. With a ladle, cover the center of the heap with the Special Hot Sauce. Take your bread and butter and mop it up spaghetti sauce–style. I add a shitload of salt just to ensure my early death by heart attack.

# RED CURRY THAI CHICKEN

## Tim King, *Soil*

I have always loved extremely hot and spicy foods. In my constant quest to find more extreme flavors and spiciness, I dabble in Thai Cuisine. The peppers and curry pastes used in these dishes not only have a unique flavor, but also add that proper kick of spicy heat to the taste buds. In this recipe I have toned down the heat aspect to make it enjoyable for all. Feel free to add or subtract the amount of curry paste to your spicy desire!

**SERVES 2 TO 3**

1 tablespoon Thai Kitchen Red Curry Paste

One 14-ounce can light coconut milk

¼ cup chopped fresh basil

One 10-ounce package frozen Thai-style vegetables

2 tablespoons canola oil

1 tablespoon brown sugar

⅓ cup chicken stock

1 pound skinless, boneless chicken breasts, cooked and cut
    into bite-size pieces

In a medium saucepan, combine curry paste and coconut milk and simmer for 5 minutes, making sure all the curry paste has dissolved.

Add all the other ingredients. Simmer for 10 to 15 minutes. Serve alone or with rice.

# HOBO STEW

### Mike Watahovich, *Ascent To The Absolute*

As a member of a temporarily unsigned band, I'm here to pass along a definite staple in the daily fight to keep metal and yourself alive! This one is appropriately titled Hobo Stew, one of my personal faves. So grab yourself an ice-cold 40-ounce. This could get messy!

First things first, round up your fellow band members and wring them of their worldly belongings. The killer part of this meal is it doesn't cost much to put together! Once everyone has contributed their fair share of dough, you need to get yourself:

**SERVES 2 TO 4**

4 or 5 medium potatoes
1 large onion
5 or 6 hot dogs or cooked sausages
Cooking oil of your choice (canola is best)
Salt and pepper

Start by washing the potatoes and cutting them into thin slices. Once cut, lay them out on a paper towel to dry. Peel the onion and slice into fairly thin slices. Hot dogs need to be cut into about ½- or 1-inch pieces. Now, if you're a guitarist, you may want to get your singer to do the cuttin'!

While all this choppin' is going on, you want to get about ¼ to ½ cup oil heated up in a frying pan. You need to be working with some high heat, so make sure you're wearing pants (hot oil can do some serious damage to your junk). Which brings me to the 40-ounce: take a moment for a swig!

Once you have the oil up to a medium-high temperature, add the potatoes and onion, occasionally stirring until they start to brown.

Add the hot dogs.

At this point, it is pretty much a judgment call as to when you're done. If you like the potatoes and hot dogs on the crunchy side, let 'em cook longer. If not, pull 'em out when they're looking about yummy, add salt, pepper, or whatever you want, and you're done.

Now depending on if you have any fat guys in the band, this is about 2 or so servings. For 4 normal-sized dudes, you can get away with about 4 servings. At this point you should be ready to crack another 40 of suds. Cheers! Here's to keeping metal and keeping you alive through the lean years!

# ROCKIN' GRILLED STUFFED LONDON BROIL

## Steve Brown, *Trixter*

**B**eing a meataterian, I love all things flesh. That said, my Rockin' Grilled Stuffed London Broil is a surefire way to satisfy the taste buds. You get the protein from the steak and mix in some cheese. What more can you ask for?

**SERVES APPROXIMATELY 4**

1 bottle good-quality cabernet sauvignon wine
2 cups chopped fresh spinach
1 cup shredded mozzarella cheese
1 cup medium to hot salsa

1¼ cups chopped fresh garlic
1½ cups olive oil
1 London broil (about 2½ pounds)

Put *Van Halen* into your stereo and crank it up.

Open up the wine and pour a glass. In the rock 'n' roll cooking world, you must always start any meal with a nice cocktail to get that buzz going.

Mix the spinach, cheese, salsa, garlic, and olive oil in a bowl.

Take another sip of wine. You should start feeling good by now.

Cut a pocket in the London broil and stuff with the spinach mixture.

Take another two sips of wine and preheat your grill for 5 minutes so it gets nice and rockin' hot.

Place the stuffed London broil on the grill with a medium heat setting for about 12 minutes. Try not to overcook the meat. It is much better on the rare side.

After grilling, place the meat on a solid cutting board and cut it into thin slices.

Serve with a salad and corn on the cob and another bottle of wine!!

Enjoy!!!

# BITTNER'S BRUTAL BREAKFAST BURRITO

## Jason Bittner, *Shadows Fall*

This is one of my favorite breakfasts because it's quick, easy, tastes great, and is full of protein, which is great after a workout.

SERVES 1

¼ pound ground turkey

1 egg

3 egg whites

1 wrap-size whole-wheat tortilla

½ cup shredded cheese

¼ cup chopped green bell pepper

Hot salsa

Brown turkey in a nonstick frying pan until cooked and golden brown. Keep warm.

Beat the egg and egg whites together in a bowl. Pour into the frying pan and scramble up until nice and fluffy.

Add the cheese and peppers to the eggs.

Place the tortilla in the microwave for 30 seconds.

Toss the egg mixture and turkey into the tortilla. Spoon on salsa and roll up.

Enjoy!

# CALIFORNIA CALAMARI RAMEN

## Lizzie Grey, *Spiders & Snakes*

If you're a musician on a budget after decades of rocking in the underground and being perpetually ignored by the major labels, here's legendary Lizzie Grey's own gourmet specialty for seafood lovers who just spent the entire week's food budget on a new set of guitar strings. Sidekick Timothy Jay gives it the official thumbs up! It's based on that prince of pastas—ramen noodles—the unique Asian delicacy that's been keeping struggling Southern California artists alive through the tough times since even before Jim Morrison made Venice Beach a cool place to hang out! Sure, sushi in the Malibu colony up the coast is where you want to be, but why settle for plain old ramen while you're waiting for that platinum album to get you there?

SERVES 2

1 pound raw squid (not the high-end prepared caps without the tentacles, we're talkin' SQUID)
2 packages ramen noodles (spicy or shrimp flavor)
1 cup diced green onions (scallions)
2 tablespoons cooking oil
Louisiana Hot Sauce (or hot sauce of your choice)

First, let's prepare the squid. Take those rubbery little guys and soak them in fresh water for a few minutes to make sure they don't have any communicable diseases. After that, separate the tentacles from the caps with a quick slice, or even by simply tearing them away. (A lot of squid you buy comes already separated.) Either way, don't throw the tentacles away, because they taste awesome. What you want to do is remove the beak from the center of the tentacle cluster by simply pushing it out with your finger. Once your tentacles have been debeaked, you can toss them back into the fresh water and concentrate on slicing the caps (which look a bit too much like condoms if left whole) into the familiar circular shape of fried calamari.

Next, boil some hot water in a large saucepan and get your ramen started (same as with any pasta). If you've never cooked ramen before, you probably have no business reading this book anyway. A unique twist to the preparation here is at the end stage, where instead of pouring the flavor packet into the water to make a soup, instead you drain the water off and pour the flavor packet onto the noodles to make sticky ramen. Set aside.

Now back to the squid. Pour cooking oil into a large skillet and turn the heat up to medium-high. Once the oil is heated up, drop your squid along with the green onions into the skillet and cook until thoroughly browned, 5 to 10 minutes depending on whether you paid the gas bill or not.

Once the squid is browned, pour in ¼ cup hot sauce and cook for a minute or 2 more. Finally, you spoon the sticky ramen into the squid skillet and, adding a few more tablespoons of hot sauce, lightly brown the squid/ramen mixture, cooking for a minute or so.

You now have prepared Spiders & Snakes California Calamari Ramen and can have your roadie (or groupie) dish it onto paper plates for all to enjoy. Chopsticks are optional.

A wonderful drink to complete this glorious repast is the classic Snakebite (a huge favorite with the Spiders & Snakes crowd). Simply combine one part lager of your choice with one part hard cider and YOU'RE BITTEN!

# LION'S SHARE PORK

## Lars Chriss, *Lion's Share*

This was my mother's signature dish when I was a kid and when we had people over for dinner. The combination of the peas, cream, onions, and melted cheese is unbelievable. So far I haven't met anyone who doesn't love this dish.

**SERVES 4**

14 ounces pork tenderloin
Salt
Ground black and white pepper
1 tablespoon butter
2 cups water
1 or 2 yellow onions
½ cup heavy cream
Grated cheese (choose your favorite)
2 cups frozen green peas

Rinse the meat and cut it into ½-inch-thick slices. Sprinkle on some salt and pepper. Coat a large frying pan in butter, add the pork, and fry it until browned.

Meanwhile, preheat the oven to 430°F.

After the pork slices are cooked, place them in an ovensafe baking dish, leaving a 1-inch margin on each side of the dish.

Turn the heat back on the frying pan and add the water, a little at a time. Stir continually, until gravy is formed.

Slice the onions and place one slice on each piece of meat. Pour the cream proportionally on each slice of meat. Top each piece with shredded cheese.

Pour the gravy around the sides of the baking dish.

Place the baking dish on the lowest oven rack for 15 to 20 minutes.

Remove the dish from the oven and pour the peas in the 1-inch wide gap between the meat and the sides of the dish.

Place back in oven for another 10 to 15 minutes.

Serve with boiled potatoes.

# THE HERMANO KENTUCKY HOT BROWN

## Dandy Brown, *Hermano*

**P**assed along to me by my mother—a Barboursville, Kentucky woman—this meal has become a weekend staple in our household. It definitely promises to stick with you for hours, and will probably knock you back into a coma for one of those long, relaxing weekend mornings. I often use a store-bought brand of biscuits, but for those without the benefit of being able to obtain these, or for those who would prefer to put that extra touch of "home-cooking" into the meal, I have also provided a basic biscuit recipe. For that extra burst of starch, I also usually prepare this meal with a side of fried potatoes, complete with onions, green peppers, and garlic. Word to the wise, though . . . do not plan on eating this if you plan on being extremely active, or if you have high cholesterol levels or a heart condition!!

SERVES 4

### GRAVY

1 pound bacon or fresh sausage
2 tablespoons all-purpose flour
¼ teaspoon salt
¼ teaspoon ground pepper
1 quart whole milk

### BISCUITS

2 cups all-purpose flour
4 teaspoons baking powder
½ teaspoon salt
3 tablespoons butter, at room temperature
¾ cup whole milk
Melted butter

◆◆◆◆◆◆◆◆◆◆◆◆◆◆◆◆◆◆◆◆◆◆◆◆◆◆◆◆◆◆◆◆◆◆◆◆◆◆◆◆◆◆◆◆◆◆◆◆◆◆◆

### Gravy Preparation

Fry the bacon in a large frying pan. While frying the bacon, mix all the remaining gravy ingredients together in a mixing bowl. Be sure to completely whip the salt, pepper, and flour into the milk, avoiding any lumps.

After the bacon has reached the desired crispness, remove it from the pan. (If using sausage, I will sometimes crumble and leave about ¼ pound of it in the pan to cook with the gravy mixture.) Do not drain or clean the pan. Add the combined gravy ingredients to the remaining oil. Cook the ingredients on low to medium heat. The trick to good gravy is to stir continuously until it has reached the desired consistency. Also, since the gravy is milk-based, stirring is critical to avoid any burning. Once the gravy has reached the desired consistency, remove immediately from the heat. Allow it to cool for 2 or 3 minutes for added thickening. Additional salt and pepper can be added to the meal upon serving to reach desired flavor.

### Biscuit Preparation

Preheat the oven to 350°F.

Mix the flour, baking powder, salt, and butter. Add milk and mix. Roll out 1-inch thick. Cut in rounds with a biscuit cutter. Reroll the scraps and cut out more biscuits. Place them on a nonstick baking sheet. Brush the tops with melted butter. Bake for about 15 minutes. You will know the biscuits are done when there is a nice brownish color covering the tops.

To serve, place 2 biscuits on a plate. Cut up the sausage or take crumbled bacon and place on top of the split biscuits. Then pour the Kentucky brown gravy over biscuits and bacon. Enjoy!

# CARIBBEAN CHICKEN SALAD

## Doro Pesch, *Warlock*

**A**ttractive women always are very careful with their health and body, and as a female singer on the road—playing more than 100 shows per year—I am very, very careful. I love chicken, turkey, and salad. Over the years, I have tried a lot of combinations, and this is the one that turned out to be my absolute favorite. It tastes good, it's healthy, and it's not so difficult to put together.

**SERVES 2**

2 cups cubed cooked chicken or turkey

3 cups cooked rice, cooled

1 cup thinly sliced celery

¼ cup chopped green bell pepper

8-ounce can crushed pineapple, drained

2 tablespoons sliced pimiento

½ cup nonfat yogurt

¼ cup mayonnaise

1½ tablespoons lemon juice

1 teaspoon curry powder

½ teaspoon salt

¼ teaspoon ground pepper

Combine chicken, rice, celery, green pepper, pineapple, and pimiento in a large bowl. In a small bowl or jar, mix together the remaining ingredients. Pour over chicken. Toss lightly until well mixed. Chill.

# MASHED POTATO SANDWICH

## Ryan Clark, *Demon Hunter*

This idea came to me in a moment of post-Thanksgiving hunger, and I've been making it for a few years now. The concept is simple, and the taste is absolutely mind blowing. Mashed potatoes have always been my favorite part of Thanksgiving dinner, and with the help of a little bread and cheese, leftovers will never be the same.

Simply take 2 slices of bread (white or whole-wheat, your choice), and throw them in the toaster. Meanwhile, take the leftover mashed potatoes out of the fridge, and throw a small serving into a microwaveable bowl. Microwave for 1 to 1½ minutes. When the bread has finished toasting, throw it on a plate and spread mashed potatoes on one of the slices (the more, the better, even if it gets messy). Place 1 slice of cheddar cheese on top of the potatoes, close the sandwich with the remaining piece of bread, and enjoy. The potatoes and bread should be hot enough to quickly melt the cheese as you begin to eat.

# SHEPHERD'S PIE

## Chris Caffery, *Savatage/Trans-Siberian Orchestra*

As a rock 'n' roll musician I usually don't get a ton of time to cook. Every once in a while, I have a day when I just feel the need to. This recipe is not only one that everyone seems to like, it is amazing for the leftover factor. Late at night, stumble home, stick it in the microwave, fun for all!!!

**PAN WILL EASILY FEED FIVE VERY HUNGRY ADULTS**

One 15-ounce box instant mashed potatoes (Hungry Jack preferred!
    Milk, water, salt, and butter or margarine required)
2 tablespoons olive oil
1 medium red onion, chopped
4 garlic cloves, chopped
1 pound lean ground beef
One 1-ounce packet onion soup mix
2 cans Campbell's Healthy Request Chunky Old-Fashioned Vegetable
    Beef Soup
1 small (7 to 10 ounces) package frozen mixed vegetables
One 8-ounce bag shredded cheese (Mexican mix preferred)*
Ground black pepper
Cayenne pepper
Chopped fresh parsley

Preheat the oven to 375°F. Prepare the mashed potatoes as directed on the box.

Heat the olive oil in a skillet over low heat. Add the onion and garlic and stir until the onions are well done.

Add the ground beef and onion soup mix. Increase the heat and brown the meat completely. Drain off the excess fat and oil.

Return the pan to the burner and add the canned soup and the vegetables. Bring the mixture to a boil. Remove from the heat and pour the entire mixture into a 9 x 13-inch baking pan. Spread evenly. Slowly cover mixture evenly with the mashed potatoes.

Cover mashed potatoes evenly with the cheese. Sprinkle black pepper and cayenne lightly over the entire casserole. Garnish with parsley.

Cover the pan with aluminum foil and bake for 15 minutes, covered. Remove the foil and cook until cheese is entirely melted or even very slightly browned. Remove from oven and let sit for 5 minutes. Kick it up a notch with your favorite hot sauce . . . BAM!!!! Serve and enjoy.

* For traditional shepherd's pie, bake without cheese and garnish.

# DALY SQUASH SOUP

## Eddie Spaghetti, *Supersuckers*

I f any of you guys like soup, try this. I have made a lot of soups, and this is by far the best and easiest! We like this recipe because it not only kicks so much ass and Q loves it, but it is easy enough for Eddie to make, cheap enough to do on a budget but fancy enough for the food snobs, AND it can be prepared for our veggie friends. Bon Appetite!

**SERVES 2**

2 medium butternut squash
Salt and pepper (Nature's Seasons is awesome)
A little oil (I like grapeseed or extra virgin olive oil)
A couple sprigs of rosemary, cilantro or any herb you like
4 slightly smashed garlic cloves
2 cups vegetable or chicken broth*
½ cup milk, half-and-half, or heavy cream (depending on your level of evilness)
¼ cup apple cider

Preheat the oven to 375°F.

Cut the squash in half lengthwise. Discard all seeds and guts. Sprinkle on some salt and pepper, and drizzle with oil. Lay the squash on a cookie sheet (cut side down) and tuck the herbs and garlic underneath (in the "bowl"). Roast in the oven for 40 to 45 minutes, until soft.**

After baking, remove the inside of the squash (the "flesh") with a spoon. Try not to burn yourself (I did) and put in a blender or food processor (sometimes I use both). Add the garlic and herbs and blend until smooth. Add 1 cup of the broth and the milk and blend some more.

Use a sieve or strainer with small holes and strain it into a soup pot. Add the remaining broth. Add the cider. Bring it to a simmer and enjoy.

◆◆◆◆◆◆◆◆◆◆◆◆◆◆◆◆◆◆◆◆◆◆◆◆◆◆◆◆◆◆◆◆◆◆◆◆◆◆◆◆◆◆◆◆◆◆◆◆◆◆◆

Alright, people, eat up! This is most delicious with crusty bread. We dig the Como kind. I don't know what that means, but it is yummy. Last night I served this with some kick-ass rosemary bread. Got the recipe out of a cooking magazine. Okay, I'll shut up now, so you can get cookin'!

XO,
The Spaghettis

\* If you are using dry broth, mix it with water first and strain it into the pot as well—we want it smooth, people.

\*\* I would also try roasting the squash on a cedar plank (if you have one) in the oven. Make sure you have a cookie sheet under it so you don't start a grease fire.

+++++++++++++++++++++++++++++++++++++++++++++++++++++++++++++++++

# JOE'S CHICKEN BOG

## Josh James, *Evergreen Terrace*

**C**hicken Bog is the jam. When consumed it gives you the strength of 1,568 men. It tastes like God, if God was a food. This is something my dad taught me how to make. My dad's name is Joe, so I called it Joe's Chicken Bog.

SERVES 2 OR 3

3 bone-in chicken breast halves
2 cups converted rice (I prefer Zatarain's Extra Long Grain Rice)
2 pounds Jimmy Dean's All-Natural Hot Pork Sausage
1 cup chopped sweet onions
Red pepper flakes (optional)

Combine 6½ cups cold water and the chicken in a large pot. Bring to a boil, reduce to a simmer, and cook until done, about 20 minutes. Remove the breasts and place on paper towels to drain. Save the broth.

Add the rice to the chicken broth and cook for about 15 minutes. Stir often. Do not overcook the rice.

Fry the sausage until almost done breaking it up as you cook. Add the onions. Mix well and continue cooking until sausage is browned and the onions are translucent. Add some red pepper flakes while the sausage cooks if you like a little spice.

Pull the chicken off the bone and place in a big bowl. Drain the rice and pour it over the chicken. Add the sausage and onions and mix well. (Do not drain the sausage—Jimmy Dean's has very little fat.)

Stir with a fork until it is all blended together.

THEN YOU STUFF.

# GO FUN STIR-FRIED CHICKEN

## Eddie Ojeda, *Twisted Sister*

When we're on the road there aren't a ton of options for healthy, good food. I love eating good food, and who doesn't? When I get back home from touring, I love making this recipe because it's fast and easy to make. It's just a great, healthy, low-calorie dish. Have a blast making this with your friends while you crank up some tunes.

**SERVES 2 TO 4**

Nonstick cooking spray (I use Pam) or 2 tablespoons vegetable oil
1 cup chopped onion (remember, there's no crying in rock 'n' roll)
¾ pound skinless, boneless lean chicken breast, chopped into bite-size chunks
3 cups assorted chopped vegetables (broccoli, cauliflower, green and red bell
   pepper chunks—you can pass on the broccoli, if you like)
4 cups bean sprouts (me like bean sprouts—it good for your colon)
¼ cup low-sodium soy sauce (or use 2 or 3 packets of the leftovers you get
   when you buy Chinese takeout, cheapskate)
3 tablespoons water

Spray a 12-inch skillet and place over medium-high heat. Add onion and cook 2 minutes or until tender, stirring occasionally (that means stir a lot, okay).

Stir in the chicken, chopped vegetables, bean sprouts, soy sauce, and water. Cover and bring to a simmer. Cook for another 2 minutes, or until the chicken is hot and vegetables are tender and crisp.

Serve with steamed brown or white rice, if desired.

# BALTI MURGH

## Nick Holmes, *Paradise Lost*

I usually vary this to suit my mood, as it's just for a basic curry. Adding more chiles, garlic, or cilantro makes it come to life. It takes a few goes to modify it to a specific taste!

I find with curry it's different strokes for different folks. Most British folk love curry, it seems, especially in the north. Maybe because it complements lager so well!

**SERVES 4**

2 tablespoons vegetable oil or ghee (clarified butter)
1 red bell pepper, cut into ½-inch squares (well, sort of)
1 green bell pepper, cut the same
4 chicken breast halves, skinned, boned, and cut into bite-size pieces
1 medium onion, cut into big pieces
Red and green chiles, seeded, deveined, and coarsely chopped*
1 teaspoon cumin seeds
1 teaspoon paprika
1 teaspoon ground turmeric
½ teaspoon ground cinnamon
A whole bunch of store-bought basic curry sauce
1 teaspoon tomato paste
Salt
1 teaspoon garam masala
Chopped fresh cilantro, for garnish

Heat a little of the oil in a wok or frying pan over high heat. Add the bell peppers and stir-fry until they go a little brown at the edges. Remove the peppers from the wok and set aside.

Put a little more oil into the wok, heat through, then add the chicken pieces and stir-fry until they are sealed and have turned white. Remove the chicken from the wok and set aside. You will need to stir fry the chicken in two or three batches, otherwise it will just stew.

Add the rest of the oil to the wok and heat through over medium heat. Add the onion, chiles, and cumin and stir-fry until the onion is translucent but not brown. Add the paprika, turmeric, and cinnamon and stir-fry for 30 seconds.

Return the chicken pieces to the wok, along with the basic curry sauce, tomato paste, and salt to taste. Bring to a simmer, then cook on a low heat for 30 minutes, or until the chicken is cooked. Add a little hot water if the sauce gets too thick. Ten minutes from the end, stir the peppers and garam masala into the sauce.

Serve in heated individual bowls. Garnish with cilantro.

*The quantity and variety of chiles is up to you. But as a guide, I would use 3 red and 3 green, fleshy chiles for medium heat. You can always add some chili powder halfway through the cooking if it's not hot enough.

# SHRIMP CLITS ON GRIT CAKES
## Balsac, *GWAR*

**B**eing the good Southern boy that I am (I live in Antarctica, you can't get any further south than that), I am a sucker for all the classic home-style dishes like chitterlings, scrapple, pig's feet, and souse. But my favorite Southern meal is a big pile o' shrimp 'n' grits. What makes my version about a hundred times better than all the others out there is that I turn my prawns into a plate of little vaginas just begging you to gobble them up. What could be better that that? Well, you could put them on a bacon, parmesan, and pepper corn grit cake, all crunchy on the outside, rich and creamy on the inside. This is the second best thing you will ever put in your mouth!

**SERVES 1**

1¾ cups chicken stock
1¾ cups half-and-half
¾ cup quick-cooking grits (your favorite brand)
4 slices thick-cut bacon
½ cup grated Parmesan cheese

Cracked black pepper
Olive oil
1 pound raw jumbo shrimp (21–25 count)
1 tablespoon sesame oil
Kosher salt
1 teaspoon sriracha sauce

## Grits

Bring the chicken stock and half-and-half to a boil in a medium saucepan. Slowly whisk in the grits. Reduce the heat and simmer for 5 minutes (or according to package directions), stirring frequently.

Cut bacon into lardons (matchstick-size strips) and cook until crisp. Save the drippings.

Stir the bacon, Parmesan, pepper to taste, and 1 tablespoon of the bacon drippings into the grits. Simmer an additional 5 to 10 minutes, until thick.

Pour the grits onto a wax paper–lined baking sheet, spread out 1-inch thick, and refrigerate until firm.

Cut the grits into 4-inch squares, then diagonally in half to form triangular cakes.

Heat a skillet over medium-high heat and add a thin layer of olive oil. Cook the grit cakes slowly until a crust forms on the bottom, flip, and cook other side.

## Shrimp

Peel, devein, and butterfly the shrimp. Cut small slit near the top of butterflied shrimp and push tail through. Marinate the shrimp in sesame oil, salt, pepper, and sriracha for at least an hour.

Heat a small amount of olive oil in a large skillet over medium-high heat. Add the shrimp and cook until they turn pink and firm, about 5 minutes. Do not overcook.

Serve with beer-braised collard greens and garnish with sriracha sauce.

# CHICKEN À LA AL

## Alan Tecchio, *Autumn Hour/Non Fiction/Hades*

Featuring HADES Persephone's Fire hot sauce.*

I enjoy making this recipe because it has my name in it! Seriously though, I love pasta and chicken, and I have always preferred vodka sauce over red sauce. This is a vodka sauce with a little kick to it thanks to the HADES hot sauce, so it has the essential flavor of vodka sauce but more punch. The HADES hot sauce is brand new to the market, but I have been making this dish for many years with various hot sauces. I created it when I was a starving musician and needed to eat well on the cheap. Quite honestly, I never learned how to make anything else! Now I am married, and my wife Beth is a far better cook than I could ever be, so I am spoiled by her amazing recipes. She still occasionally lets me whip this one up though!

SERVES 2

1 pound skinless, boneless chicken breasts

1 cup all-purpose flour

10 tablespoons olive oil

1 medium onion, chopped

4 slices prosciutto, chopped

½ cup vodka

One 15-ounce can crushed tomatoes

2 tablespoons HADES "Persephone's Fire" hot sauce (or your favorite)

½ cup grated Romano cheese

½ cup grated Parmigiano cheese

½ cup heavy cream

4 tablespoons (½ stick) butter

Coat the chicken breasts in the flour. Heat ½ cup of the olive oil in a frying pan over medium heat and brown the chicken on each side for 6 to 7 minutes. Take out the chicken and drain the oil out of the pan. Cut the chicken into slices.

Heat the remaining 2 tablespoons olive oil in the pan over medium heat. Add the onion and prosciutto and cook, stirring, for 8 minutes. Add the vodka and cook, scraping bits from the bottom of the pan, for about 2 minutes. Add the tomatoes and cook over low heat for 30 minutes.

Add the hot sauce, sliced chicken, Romano, Parmigiano, cream, and butter and simmer for an additional 20 minutes.

*Order from www.frommildtowild.com.

# RED FANG PAD THAI

## Aaron, *Red Fang*

**W**hy pad thai? Because it usually sucks in restaurants, and it is surprisingly cheap and easy to make at home. And it's good. Red Fang is like a supermarket—we're all about high quality and low prices. Special thanks go to my friend Chris Rabilwongse (yes, that is his real name) for teaching me this recipe.

Prep all your ingredients ahead of time (chop your green onions, cut the protein into bite-size pieces, make your tamarind sauce, etc.), and have them at the ready. The cooking goes very fast, so you need everything prepared and near you before you start throwing things in the pan.

Green onions (scallions), 2-inch cuts on the bias
Protein of your choice (fried tofu, chicken, shrimp, whatever)
Tamarind sauce
Pad thai noodles
Vegetable oil
Fish sauce (from the bottle)
Toasted red pepper flakes
Eggs (1 per serving)
Bean sprouts
Crushed peanuts
Cilantro leaves
Lime wedges
Sugar

To make the tamarind sauce, cut a ½-inch slice from a block of tamarind paste. Add to approximately 1 cup water in a saucepan and simmer until paste has dissolved. Add enough sugar to balance the extreme sourness of the tamarind.

Open a 9-ounce package of fresh pad thai noodles (available at most Asian markets) into a colander in the sink. Run hot water over noodles to separate.

Okay, let's cook this shit!! These instructions are for one serving at a time.

Heat some oil in wok or skillet. Throw in your protein, a little splash of tamarind sauce (start with about 2 tablespoons), 1 squirt of fish sauce, and some red pepper flakes. Cook until the protein is done, then clear a little space in the pan, and scramble 1 egg in there.

Grab about one-quarter of the noodles from the colander and throw them in the pan.

Add 3 to 5 healthy squirts of fish sauce (to taste) and an equal amount of tamarind sauce. Cook until the noodles have softened. If the noodles look too dry, add a little water.

Once the noodles have softened (takes about 15 seconds), throw in a handful of bean sprouts, green onions, peanuts, and more red pepper flakes.

Toss together. Transfer to serving bowl.

Top with more ground peanuts, cilantro, and serve with a wedge of fresh lime and Singha beer.

# VEGETARIAN TOFU PAD THAI

## James Heatley, *The Answer*

**T**his is one of my favorite dishes from Thailand. So much so, in fact, that once I actually had it for lunch and dinner in the same day on Ko Samui! For lunch I had it in a high-class restaurant, and the dish alone cost around £25. Later that day I had it from a stall in the streets of Chaweng, and it cost less than a £1. But both were equally good. This is a somewhat Irish take on it. I never use an actual recipe, just make it up as I go. Hope you like it as much as I do.

This dish doesn't take long to cook, and the vegetables should be served quite crunchy but very hot. So before you start cooking, it is good to have all your ingredients washed and prepared, otherwise you are going to have to multitask and that's never good!

SERVES 3 OR 4

Small handful of peanuts (your preference—I use jalapeño-flavored peanuts)

One 8-ounce package egg noodles (you can also use rice noodles)

Sea salt

1 tablespoon sesame oil

Soy sauce

3 tablespoons peanut oil

2 garlic cloves, thinly sliced

Thumb-size piece fresh ginger, peeled and finely chopped

½ medium onion, finely chopped

5 ounces marinated tofu pieces

4 ounces canned baby corn

4 ounces snow peas

4 ounces mushrooms, chopped

1 fresh red chile, seeded and sliced

2 scallions (that's green onions or Irish spring onions), sliced

4 ounces bean sprouts

2 tablespoons pad thai noodle sauce (your favorite brand)

½ cup pineapple chunks (fresh or canned—whatever you can get)

Ground black pepper

1 lime

1 bunch of fresh cilantro, leaves taken off and stalks chopped

Put your nuts (pardon the pun) in a mortar and crush them with the pestle for 5 seconds. You don't want them to be dust. It's the crunchy bits that make it.

Cook your egg noodles in a large saucepan of boiling water (with a little sea salt), according to the packet instructions. Drain the noodles well, then put them in a large bowl and toss them with the sesame oil and a splash of soy sauce. Set them aside.

Heat the peanut oil in a wok or a large frying pan and stir-fry the garlic, ginger, and onion for 1 minute. Add your tofu and fry for another minute, until the edges of the tofu start to brown. Next, add the baby corn, snow peas, and mushrooms, along with the chile slices (keep a little aside for garnish) and continue to stir-fry quickly for another 2 minutes.

Add the scallions, bean sprouts, and pad thai noodle sauce, and stir-fry for another 2 minutes.

Toss in the drained noodles, along with the pineapple, 1 to 2 tablespoons soy sauce, and freshly ground black pepper. Squeeze half of the lime over the noodles, and sprinkle with fresh chopped cilantro.

Continue to cook over a high heat for 2 minutes more, stirring well until all the ingredients are well mixed and heated through.

Divide it out into bowls and quickly add a little sprinkle of red chile, chopped cilantro, a generous coating of crushed peanuts, and a wedge of lime on the side.

Serve at once with a lovely Thai beer.

# CHICKEN PAPRIKASH

## John Corabi, *The Scream/Mötley Crüe/Union*

I sent this recipe, well, because . . . my ex-wife used to make this, and I recall the first time she made it, thinking "WTF . . . sour cream and stewed tomatoes on chicken . . . That's going to taste like ASS!" Well, she put it on the table, and I tasted it and FREAKED!!!! It was really great! So later, after we divorced, and I was dating, I used to pull this recipe out when I wanted to impress a girl with my prowess in the kitchen. You know, the big rock star with the cool pad and sports car and the tight leather pants is making the girl some gourmet fancy-ass meal, and it always worked . . . to some degree. Yeah, I got some, but it wasn't until later, because I usually ate soooo much, I would just fall into a food coma and wake up and find I'd actually married the girl and we were now in the process of getting divorced, and I had to give her HALF!!!! Which is a whole other book . . . LOL.

**SERVES 2 VERY HUNGRY PEOPLE**

1 to 1½ pounds skinless, boneless chicken breasts
1 green bell pepper, chopped
2 small scallions (green onions), chopped
Italian seasoning
Paprika—hence the name, Chicken Paprikash
Garlic powder
Salt and pepper
One 14.5-ounce can stewed tomatoes
1 cup sour cream
One 16-ounce bag egg noodles

Boil water for the noodles.

Cut the chicken into bite-size pieces, and put them into a large nonstick skillet with the green pepper and scallions and a few drops of water. Cook the chicken until the meat is white throughout, then drain off excess water. Add Italian seasoning, paprika, and garlic powder, salt, and pepper to taste. Add the tomatoes and sour cream and cook, covered, on a low flame, stirring occasionally.

Add noodles to the boiling water and cook according to the package directions. When the noodles are done, drain, rinse and mix them with the chicken.

Personally I love this stuff, but I also think it's better the day after, when everything has had a chance to blend, so I've been known to make this the day before. BE-WARE! If you cook like I do, IT'S MESSY!!!! But worth it.

Peace,
Crabby

# MOM'S STUFFING

## Charlie Benante, *Anthrax*

This stuffing has been in my family for years; it could be 100+ years old. We've been having it at Thanksgiving for as long as I can remember. My sisters and I would wait for it every year—we were hooked. My mom gave me the recipe a few years ago and my first attempt at it was a success. I stay pretty close to the recipe but I do prefer it with turkey. I try to make it at least twice a year, I should make it more . . . it's that good.

### THIS WILL FEED EVERYONE YOU INVITE OVER FOR DINNER

1½ cups rice

8 large onions

2 pounds carrots

1½ pounds celery

1 package small mushrooms (whole or sliced)

12 tablespoons (1½ sticks) butter

Olive oil

1 pound ground beef or turkey

One 28-ounce can crushed tomatoes

Generous handful of chopped parsley

3 large eggs

1½ cups bread crumbs

1 cup grated Parmigiano cheese

Dash of salt and pepper

Cook your rice first and let sit.

Slice the onions in a food processor and put 'em in a bowl. Slice the carrots in the food processor and add 'em to the bowl. Slice the celery in the food processor, and add em to the bowl. Add the sliced mushrooms, or if you bought whole mushrooms, slice them up too.

Now, get a big pot (a 12-quart pot should do it) and heat the butter and 2 capfuls of olive oil over medium heat. Add the onions, carrots, celery, and mushrooms. Cook that for 20 minutes.

Preheat the oven to 375°F.

Now grab a big skillet and cook the meat over medium heat for about 5 minutes. Once the meat is browned, throw it in the big pot. Add the cooked rice, tomatoes, and parsley to the big pot.

Stir occasionally so it doesn't burn. Scrape the mixture into a large bowl. Let it sit for 25 minutes, to cool.

Crack your eggs into the stuffing and mix in well. Add the bread crumbs and cheese and mix it all in. Add salt and pepper if you like.

Get a 13 x 9-inch pan and spray it with Pam or something like that. Put the stuffing in there (you may have some leftovers so you may wanna have another pan on hand). Bake for 35 minutes or until brown.

That's it, ENJOY!

# CHUCK'S EVIL CHILI

## Chuck Schuldiner, *Death*

**M**y son Chuck was cooking from an early age, and he followed a long list of Schuldiner men who were excellent cooks, including his father, his older brother, and his nephew. Chuck wasn't satisfied with just making food, he added to it with creativity, amassing a huge collection of herbs and spices. He also created his own recipes as he went along, some of which I use. When he had a newsletter sent out to the fans, he included some of his own recipes in it, and the fans wrote that they used them, they loved it, still writing to me as new ones discover them on the internet, asking for the brand names of the foods Chuck used so theirs would taste just like his. Everything was from scratch, fresh vegetables only, no perservatives added. He just loved to cook, saying if he were not a musician, he would be a chef.

He was very much into healthy cooking, inside and outside at the grill. When he was in town he would cook great dinners at his house and we always ate at the table, no TV trays at Chuck's house, just as we did as he was growing up. His bandmates, his family, his friends, we all enjoyed eating at Chuck's house.

—Jane Schuldiner

SERVES 2 TO 4

Two 15-ounce cans pink beans
One 15-ounce can black beans
3 tablespoons chili powder
2 tablespoons Cajun spice blend
1 tablespoon Mrs. Dash's Table Blend
2 capfuls Worcestershire sauce
2 capfuls Jamaican jerk marinade
Few drops of Chef Paul Prudhommes
    Magic Pepper Sauce
Dash of Italian seasoning

4 fresh tomatoes, diced
½ can (10.75 ounce) condensed tomato
    soup
1 cup water
3 celery stalks, sliced
1 red onion, chopped
1 red bell pepper, chopped
1 green bell pepper, chopped
1 pound ground hamburger meat,
    cooked (optional)

Dump everything into a pot and cook for 2 hours over medium-low heat. Freeze unused portions for future quickies.

# CAYENNE BOURBON SALMON

## Todd Smith, *Dog Fashion Disco/Knives Out!*

**M**y family and I used to make this dish all the time in the summer when we're hanging out at the family beach house. The best thing about this recipe is that it only calls for 4 teaspoons of bourbon. While you're waiting for dinner to cook you can pound down the rest of the bourbon to pass the time!!

SERVES 2

1 cup pineapple juice
½ cup soy sauce
½ cup brown sugar
4 teaspoons bourbon
2 teaspoons black pepper

2 teaspoons cayenne pepper
1 teaspoon minced garlic
1¼ pounds salmon fillets
Freshly grated Parmesan cheese

Combine the pineapple juice, soy sauce, brown sugar, bourbon, black pepper, cayenne, and garlic in a large measuring cup or small bowl. Lay the salmon fillets on a baking tray and pour a generous amount of the pineapple marinade on the salmon. Let the fillets sit for 15 minutes in the fridge before you cook.

Preheat the oven to 350°F.

Bake the salmon for 12 to 15 minutes, or until flaky and center is cooked thoroughly. Sprinkle freshly grated Parmesan. Serve with sides of whole grain rice or pasta and asparagus.

Bon appétit!!

# ENCORES

# APPLE AND RAISIN CRUMBLE

## Neil Cooper, *Therapy*

I thought about turning this into a more rock 'n' roll recipe by adding alcohol, etc. Then I thought, *You know what? Screw it. It's great as it is!*

You can't beat getting back from tour to home-cooked bits and bobs like this. I tend to chuck the radio on and listen to Derby County's away games whilst pottering about in the kitchen making this sort of stuff. Give it a go, you'll love it.

SERVES 4

**FILLING**

A couple of handfuls of raisins

Boiling water

Jack Daniel's

Coca-Cola

1 pound Bramley apples (or your favorite baking apple), peeled, cored, and sliced

A smidge of butter

6 tablespoons light brown sugar

A pinch of ground cinnamon

A pinch of ground ginger

**TOPPING**

8 tablespoons (1 stick) butter

2 cups all-purpose flour

A pinch of ground ginger

¼ cup Demerara sugar or raw cane sugar

Chuck the raisins in a small bowl filled with boiling water. This helps plump 'em up.

While you give the raisins a minute, you might as well pour yourself a stiff Jack Daniel's and Coke. This'll help things run much smoother.

Whack the oven onto 350°F.

Drain the water from the raisins. Put the apples and raisins into a greased, oven-proof baking dish and dot with butter. Mix the brown sugar and cinnamon together and sprinkle on top of the fruit. Then sprinkle a pinch of ginger on top.

For the topping, put the butter, flour, ginger, and half the Demerara sugar into a bowl. Rub the butter into the flour until you have a bread crumb–like mixture.

Chuck the topping over the fruit and press down lightly with a spoon. Scatter the remaining sugar on top.

Chuck it in the oven for 45 minutes, or until the top is golden and crisp.

Serve hot with vanilla ice cream. Smashing!

Cheers

# LIME GELATIN MOLD

## Tom Davies, *Nebula*

It's all shades of wrong but tastes so good. None of these ingredients should be mixed together, but somehow they create a very psychedelic-looking and tasting dessert. Highly recommended.

SERVES 6

One 3-ounce package lime Jell-O
½ cup mayonnaise
2 tablespoons lemon juice
¼ teaspoon salt
One 15-ounce can fruit cocktail, drained
3 ounces cream cheese, diced
¼ cup chopped walnuts
1 banana, diced

Mix up Jell-O according to the package, beat until frothy, pour into a greased pan, and put in the freezer until almost set.

In a small bowl, beat together the mayonnaise, lemon juice, and salt. Transfer the Jell-O to a large bowl, add the mayonnaise mixture, and beat lightly until frothy.

Fold in the rest of the ingredients. Pour into a greased 6- to 8-cup mold and refrigerate until set.

# EXTRA RICH CHOCOLATE PECAN PIE

### Jacob Lynam, *Lynam*

This is my favorite recipe by far because it combines two of my favorite things. I'm a total chocolate junkie. Being from the deep South, I love pecans, so this definitely gets the job done. I make this pie every Thanksgiving and Christmas (and any other time I get the chance).

**SERVES 8**

1 cup semisweet chocolate chips
(one 6-ounce bag)
⅔ cup evaporated milk
2 tablespoons butter
2 large eggs
1 cup sugar

2 tablespoons unbleached all-purpose flour
¼ teaspoon salt
1 teaspoon vanilla extract
1 cup chopped pecans
1 unbaked 9-inch pie shell

Preheat the oven to 375°F.

Combine the chocolate chips, evaporated milk, and butter in a small saucepan. Cook over low heat, stirring constantly, until mixture is smooth and creamy.

Combine the eggs, sugar, flour, salt, vanilla, and pecans in a bowl and mix well.

Gradually stir the chocolate mixture into the egg mixture, blending well, and pour into the unbaked pie shell.

Bake for 40 minutes, or until the filling is set.

Cool on a wire rack.

Enjoy.

# NORWEGIAN APPLECAKE

### Liv Kristine, *Leaves' Eyes*

**S**ince I moved to Germany twelve years ago, it has become very important to me to serve traditional Norwegian dishes. This cake is my favorite sweet dish. I just love the scent of apples and cinnamon in the cold seasons. It's uncomplicated and easily baked and tastes like cinnamon heaven. My version is both gluten- and lactose-free, as I have to be aware of this myself.

**SERVES 6 TO 8**

### CAKE

3 large eggs
1 cup minus 2 tablespoons cane sugar (or ¾ cup regular
    granulated sugar plus 2 tablespoons honey)
⅔ cup melted butter (soy butter for lactose-free)
1 cup all-purpose flour (cornmeal for gluten-free)
Pinch of vanilla sugar
1 teaspoon baking powder
1 teaspoon ground cinnamon

### TOPPING

3 apples (not too ripe) from the garden or whole food store
    (not the shiny, nontasting ones)
Sugar
Ground cinnamon

Preheat the oven to 350°F. Grease an 8-inch round cake pan, preferably one with a loose bottom.

◆◆◆◆◆◆◆◆◆◆◆◆◆◆◆◆◆◆◆◆◆◆◆◆◆◆◆◆◆◆◆◆◆◆◆◆◆◆◆◆◆◆◆◆◆◆◆◆◆

Beat the eggs with the cane sugar. Stir in the melted butter. Whisk together the flour, vanilla sugar, baking powder, and cinnamon. Fold the dry ingredients into the eggs. Pour the batter into the pan.

Peel, core, and slice the apples. Arrange slices on top of the cake mix in two circles, one apple slice covering half of the following one. Sprinkle cinnamon-sugar mix on top.

Bake for 40 minutes on the middle rack, until the top of cake is nicely browned and a sharp knife inserted in the middle of the cake comes out dry. Serve with whipped cream, if preferred.

Good luck, and *god appetitt!*
Liv

# OREO CHEESECAKE

## Dennis Pavia, *Diecast*

**I** love this recipe because it is very easy to make, delicious, and will give you the energy you need to endure the mosh pits! Inspired by Kraft Foods' Philly Oreo Cheesecake recipe.

**SERVES 8**

One 18-ounce package Oreo cookies
¼ cup melted butter or margarine
Four 8-ounce packages cream cheese, softened

1 cup sugar
1 teaspoon vanilla extract
¾ cup sour cream
4 large eggs

Preheat oven to 325°F.

Place 30 of the cookies in a plastic zipper bag. Flatten the bag to remove excess air, then seal. Finely crush cookies by rolling a rolling pin across the bag. Pour the crushed cookies into a bowl. Add butter; mix well. Press firmly onto the bottom of a 13 by 9-inch baking pan.

Beat the cream cheese, sugar, and vanilla in a large bowl with a mixer until well blended. Add sour cream; mix well. Add the eggs, one at a time, beating just until blended after each.

Chop the remaining cookies in a food processor. Stir 1½ cups into the batter.

Pour the batter into the crust and top with remaining chopped cookies.

Bake for 45 minutes, or until the center is almost set. Let it cool slowly by first turning the oven off. Wait 15 minutes, then slightly open the oven. Wait 15 minutes more and remove from the oven. Let it cool completely. Refrigerate for 4 hours. This process will help prevent cracking.

# PECAN PIE

## John Bundy, *Naam*

**P**ie is awesome, especially pecan pie. It's a real treat that you can't eat often for obvious reasons, but damn, it's so good! This is a recipe that I've perfected over the past twelve or so years, only breaking it out for Thanksgiving and Xmas. It's a Southern tradition that I'm proud of and seems to capture the soul of real Southern cooking. I can't even say I have much of a sweet tooth, but pecan pie brings it out in all of us.

**SERVES 8**

1 cup dark corn syrup

3 large or jumbo eggs

¾ cup granulated sugar

¼ cup brown sugar

2 tablespoons butter, melted

1 teaspoon pure vanilla extract (not imitation)

Pinch of ground cinnamon

Pinch of ground nutmeg

1½ cups chopped pecans, about 6 ounces

1 unbaked 9-inch deep-dish pie crust

Preheat the oven to 350°F.

Stir the corn syrup, eggs, sugars, butter, vanilla, cinnamon, and nutmeg together in a large bowl, until well blended. Mix in the pecans. Pour into the pie crust.

Bake on the center rack for 55 to 60 minutes. Turn off the oven and let the pie sit inside for 10 to 15 minutes. Check pie's center with a knife to ensure a solid mixture. Once pie is no longer runny, remove it from the oven, and set out to cool. Let cool for 2 hours.

# CHOCKA-CORN

## Ryan Roxie, *Alice Cooper*

For those of you who don't know what a speedball is . . . good. It's probably better that ya don't. That way, you keep living the good life, and I don't have to explain just how dark the "dark side" of rock 'n' roll can get. I've been lucky enough in my career to actually avoid speedballs (*and* speed freaks for that matter!), but this recipe that I am about to bestow on you might even send the speediest of speed freaks running to their nearest Betty Ford clinic in search of a cure. And the only cure is more Chocka-Corn.

In elaborate, technical terms, Chocka-Corn combines two opposite tastes that metamorphose into what scientists can only describe as "delicious." Now, I'm no scientist, but after discovering this incredibly important combination I feel I should be awarded some sort of honorary doctorate somewhere. Does G.I.T. have a Ph.D. program?! Didn't think so.

The equation is simple: Combine sugar and salt. BUT, masking the sugar in the form of chocolate-covered raisins, and hiding the salt innocently enough in a batch of heavily salted popcorn is pure genius.

1 bag microwave popcorn (if ya gotta go ol' school, use Jiffy Pop)
One 10-ounce box (at the very least, you wimp!!) chocolate-covered raisins
   (Raisinettes being the brand of choice . . . wait a second, are there any
   other brands?!)

Carefully read the directions on how to pop the popcorn, and then do so.

Open the box of Raisinettes (or whatever bargain basement brand you were able to salvage up).

Keep 'em separated (hey, just like the Offspring song!) until it is time to experience the bittersweet—I mean salty-sweet—sensation of a lifetime, or at least the duration of whatever crappy DVD you just rented. Place popcorn in mouth (hopefully yours, unless it's one of "those" DVDs) and then follow it with a Raisinette. Let both mix and melt until it becomes a raging, ravishing, taste-bud orgy inside you (just like the DVD you just rented!!).

## The Epilogue

Probably one of the easiest desserts to cook up in this book, unless someone has simply listed "Candy Bar" as a recipe. But trust me (no, not f**k you in Los Angeles–talk), really trust me that this dish will save your life. It will literally SAVE YOUR LIFE. And next time someone says, "Tell Me Something Good," don't think Chaka Kahn, think Chocka-Corn!!! Actually no, don't think of either, think of me, Ryan Roxie, and send me a dollar for saving your life.

About the author of this recipe: Roxie spends too much of his spare time at home or on tour buses watching bad movies from the 1980s (can you say *St. Elmo's Fire* or *Fletch Lives*?), so his experience with chocolate and popcorn is both justified and mystifying.

# GRANNY IX'S ALCOHOL-INFUSED NEW ORLEANS–STYLE BREAD PUDDING

## Mike Williams, *Eyehategod*

N eed I say more about why I like this dessert recipe? Sugar and liquor go together like Hanneman and King!

### BREAD PUDDING

8 tablespoons (1 stick) unsalted
   butter, plus more for the pan

3 to 5 cups day-old, stale French
   bread, cubed or crumbled

2 cups light brown sugar

9 large eggs

1 cup granulated sugar

Pinch of salt

1 teaspoon vanilla extract

¼ to ½ cup booze (your preference)

One 12-ounce can evaporated milk

3 cups whole milk

1 bottle of vodka

2 cups raw sugar

### SAUCE

1 cup sugar

½ cup water

2 to 3 teaspoons cornstarch

1 bottle of rum or bourbon

Butter a 12 by 9-inch baking pan and fill about halfway with bread. Sprinkle some brown sugar all over.

In a bowl, mix the eggs (beaten like your cheating ex-wife), along with the granu-lated sugar, salt, vanilla, and life-sustaining booze (about ¼ cup or more, depending on your taste).

In a saucepan, combine the evaporated milk, whole milk, and butter. Scald milk over low heat until skin forms. Remove saucepan from heat and slowly add about half of the heated milk from the saucepan into the bowl of egg mixture. Stir, then return the entire mixture back into the saucepan. Pour contents of saucepan over the bread in the pan.

If you'd like, add your choice of pecans, bananas, raisins, or almonds at this time. Allow the mixture to soak into the bread (about an hour or so; take this time to down the bottle of vodka) and add more bread if needed to absorb remaining liquid. The longer the soak, the better. You want it to be a bit soupy, so don't add bread if you don't need to.

Preheat the oven to 325°F.

Cover the pudding with at least ½ inch of brown sugar, then top with a solid layer of raw sugar. Fill a large roasting pan with about ½ to ¾ inch water, and place the pan of bread pudding inside (this will keep it moist). Bake for an hour or so, until top is brown, crisp, and bubbling. It's finished when you can stick a cold butter knife in the center and nothing sticks to it.

## Sauce

Heat the sugar, water, and cornstarch (use as needed to thicken sauce) over medium heat and cook until the sugar is dissolved. Don't forget the liquor!! Add to taste and stir until the sauce thickens. When the bread pudding is done, pour the finished sauce over top. Eat up!

For praline bread pudding, add 1 cup pecans. For rum-raisin bread pudding, add 1 cup raisins.

# HIGHLY DOUBTFUL TEACAKE WITH VERY SUSPICIOUS CREME

## Emilie Autumn

What makes this teacake so very "doubtful" is the addition of fresh lavender, the historical meaning for which is distrust. So, be careful whom you share your cake with . . .

Please feel quite free to use the lavender you've been growing in your yard for this teacake, just be sure there are no pesticides present.

| | |
|---|---|
| 1 cup milk | 1 cup sugar |
| 3 tablespoons chopped fresh lavender flowers | 1 teaspoon pure vanilla extract |
| 2 cups all-purpose flour | 2 large organic eggs |
| 1½ teaspoons baking powder | Confectioners' sugar, for garnish |
| ¼ teaspoon salt | Fresh or candied lavender sprigs, (recipe follows) |
| 6 tablespoons (¾ stick) butter, softened | Very Suspicious Creme for garnish |

Lightly grease a 9 x 5–inch loaf pan and dust it with flour to prevent the cake from sticking when you try to release it from the pan later on, an occurrence that would undoubtedly send you hurtling toward the edge of a cliff at an even greater speed than that which you are used to traveling at.

In any case! After greasing and flouring, kindly preheat your oven to 325°F. In a small saucepan, heat the milk. Add the chopped lavender and bring almost to a boil, removing from the heat before the milk begins to scald. Let the milk and lavender get to know each other, steeping until cool.

Sift the flour, baking powder, and salt together in a bowl. In another bowl, thrash the butter about until it is light and creamy. Gradually add the sugar, vanilla, and the eggs, one at a time, thrashing even more until the whole mess is light and fluffy, a lovely pale yellow, and much prettier than you ever imagined raw eggs had any right to be.

Add your dry ingredients and lavender milk to the butter mixture, alternating between each addition, and mix until batter is just blended, but no longer (your rats won't mind a dense, tough teacake, but everybody else will).

Spoon the flowery goodness into your prepared loaf pan and bake for 50 minutes or until a wooden skewer inserted into the center of the cake comes out clean. Leave your masterpiece to cool in the pan for 5 minutes, then remove to a wire rack to cool completely. Once done, dust your cake with confectioners' sugar and garnish with sprigs of fresh or candied lavender.

Serve your Highly Doubtful Teacake with a generous dollop of Very Suspicious Creme, which you will bring into being as follows.

### VERY SUSPICIOUS CREME

8 ounces cream cheese
1 tablespoon heavy cream
½ teaspoon chopped fresh lavender flowers
3 tablespoons confectioners' sugar
1 teaspoon pure vanilla extract

Blend the cream cheese with the heavy cream until smooth and fluffy (more fluffiness). Gently fold in the lavender, confectioners' sugar, and vanilla, incorporating until silky and very suspicious looking. Serve with teacakes of all sorts, but especially with highly doubtful ones.

I hope your mad tea party is to die for.

# DEATH BY CHOCOLATE

Steve Blaze, *Lillian Axe*

I love this recipe because my wife and I are chocolate fanatics, and this dish contains different textures of what we love. Creamy pudding, chewy brownies, and crunchy candy with a wonderful layer of whipped topping! This recipe always gets the highest dessert ranking at all family reunions and food-related functions! So good, it's hard to get through making it without devouring the ingredients with my special assistant, Chef Jude—my five-month-old son and talented apprentice.

**SERVES 8**

One 18-ounce box family-size brownie mix
One 3.9-ounce package instant chocolate pudding
3 Heath or Skor candy bars or half a bag of Heath pieces (you can find this
    by the chocolate chips)
One 16-ounce container whipped topping

Prepare the brownie mix as directed.

Prepare the pudding as directed.

Crush the candy bars into small pieces if not using the precrushed pieces.

After brownies have cooled, cut into small squares.

In a deep bowl or trifle dish, layer brownie pieces, pudding, whipped topping, and candy bar pieces. Repeat layers, reserving enough whipped topping and candy bar pieces to top the dessert.

This dessert should be served in a clear bowl or trifle dish so everyone can see its chocolatey ability to kill you by chocolate overdose!

# FAIR TRADE VEGAN AVOCADO FUDGE

## Mark "Barney" Greenway, *Napalm Death*

If there are two things that are a big part of my life, it's the veggie/vegan dietary lifestyle and, yeah, avocados. Can't get enough of them, which may indeed make me a very boring prospect, but I care not. I just love things that sound like they would never go together—just like chili and chocolate. The first time I tried this recipe, I nearly exploded with joy! Plus it's fair trade, which everybody should really be doing, shouldn't they?

**I COULD EAT THIS ALL MYSELF**

8 tablespoons (1 stick) vegan/soy margarine

1 ripe avocado (soft to the point where you can push in your finger a little way, but not sloppy)

1 teaspoon pure vanilla extract

1 cup unsweetened cocoa

3 cups confectioners' sugar

⅓ cup chopped walnuts (optional)

In a saucepan, melt the margarine over low heat. That's LOW heat, people (I know none of you have patience or restraint).

Once the margarine is melted, puree with the avocado in a food processor or blender until perfectly smooth. Be sure there are no visible remnants of avocado left, as, er, the point is it's not a vegetable-flavored fudge as such. You're just meant to get the creamy richness of the avocado taste.

Return the mixture to the saucepan over very low heat (you getting it now?) and add the vanilla, cocoa, and sugar, adding the sugar a portion at a time. Once all the sugar has been added, the mixture should be thick—that's the beauty of science. Add the walnuts if desired, and transfer to a loaf pan. Refrigerate until firm but moist.

Now, be patient! As this is nondairy it may be a long, old wait, but it will be worth it. Have I ever lied to you? Now stuff it into your face and eat with nil decorum.

# MINI CHEESECAKE TARTS

## Ronny Munroe, *Metal Church*

I love this recipe so much because it has a lot of things I already like, it's easy to make, and I don't feel so guilty about eating sweets when I'm dieting before a tour because they're small.

**SERVES 12**

One 14-ounce box graham crackers
Two 8-ounce packages cream cheese
2 large eggs
1 cup sugar
1 teaspoon vanilla extract
Toppings: strawberry, blueberry, cherry, or fudge; vanilla wafers, Oreo cookies, or both

Preheat the oven to 350°F.

Stuff as many broken graham crackers as you can into a food processor and chop until they reach a fine consistency. Generously grease a 12-cup muffin pan and line each cup with the ground graham crackers. To flatten evenly, put some plastic wrap on the bottom of a small cup and press down into and on the sides of each muffin cup.

In a mixer, mix the cream cheese, eggs, sugar, and vanilla. Pour the mix into each cup, halfway up.

Bake for 20 minutes, pull out, and top with your favorite topping. I like them after they have only cooled for a minute or two. Eat and refrigerate any leftovers (if there are any!).

These rock!

◆◆◆◆◆◆◆◆◆◆◆◆◆◆◆◆◆◆◆◆◆◆◆◆◆◆◆◆◆◆◆◆◆◆◆◆◆◆◆◆◆◆◆◆

# THE BEST BLUEBERRY MUFFINS

## Paul Burnette, *Darkest Hour*

There's nothing more rewarding in the kitchen than freshly baked bread. These muffins really are the best. Since I've been making these at home I've turned into a muffin snob, and will no longer eat greasy, prepackaged gas station mounds of partially hydrogenated high fructose bready garbage. Stay out of my yard!

**SERVES 8**

8 tablespoons (1 stick) butter, at room temerature

1 cup sugar (or a bit less, depending on taste)

2 large eggs

1 teaspoon vanilla extract

2 teaspoons baking powder

¼ teaspoon salt

2½ cups blueberries (smash ½ cup with fork)

2 cups all-purpose flour

½ cup milk

1 tablespoon sugar mixed with ¼ teaspoon ground nutmeg, for the topping

Grease muffin cups, if needed, or line with papers. Preheat the oven to 375°F.

Stir the butter until creamy. Stir in the sugar until the mixture is pale and fluffy. Stir in the eggs, one at a time. Stir in the vanilla, baking powder, and salt.

Smash ½ cup of the blueberries and stir into the mixture.

Fold in half the flour with rubber spatula. Fold in half the milk. Fold in the remaining flour and milk. Fold in the rest of the blueberries.

Drop the batter into the muffin cups. Sprinkle with the sugar-nutmeg mixture.

Bake for 25 minutes or until golden brown.

Cool the muffins 10 minutes before removing from the pan.

# BANANA POUND CAKE

## Jamey Jasta, *Hatebreed*

I had just gotten back from tour, and I hadn't seen or spent any really good time with my daughter in over three months. This was just before her fourth birthday. It was a cold, rainy, dreary day, so we couldn't really do anything outdoors, and she didn't want to leave the house anyway. We had about four or five bananas that looked overly ripe, and I didn't want them to go to waste, so I figured I would make a protein shake or a smoothie with them, but my daughter mentioned we should bake a cake for her mom. So I looked in a bunch of cookbooks we had lying around the pantry, and I found a pound cake recipe that I altered by adding the overly ripe bananas. The end result was an awesome pound cake that my daughter and her mom loved! Now I make it for her on special occasions. It's not too good to eat a lot of it or make it too often because it's very rich and fattening! I explained to my daughter that it was called a pound cake because it used a pound of butter and a pound of sugar. That's what makes it so rich. Here's my recipe—enjoy!

SERVES 6

1 pound organic butter (4 sticks), softened

3 cups sugar

6 large free-range organic eggs

3 cups cake flour

½ teaspoon baking soda

1 teaspoon baking powder

½ teaspoon salt

3 or 4 really soft, overly ripe bananas

2 teaspoons pure vanilla extract

½ cup buttermilk

Preheat the oven to 325°F. Grease and flour the bottom and sides of a 10-inch tube or Bundt pan.

In a large bowl, cream together butter and sugar with an electric mixer on high speed until light and fluffy.

Add the eggs, one at a time, beating well after each. Set aside.

Sift together the flour, baking soda, baking powder, and salt in a separate bowl. In another bowl, mash together the bananas, vanilla, and buttermilk. Add dry and wet alternately to butter mixture, beginning and ending with dry. Mix by hand, just enough to blend thoroughly without excess beating. Spread the batter into the prepared pan.

Bake for 50 to 60 minutes, until a sharp knife inserted all the way down comes out clean. Let cool for 10 minutes in the pan, then turn out onto a plate. Cool completely before slicing.

My daughter's mom loves when I add a handful of chocolate chips for an extra yummy treat!

# VANCOUVER LASAGNA

## Burton C. Bell, *Fear Factory*

This recipe literally came to me in a dream I had during a restful sleep. In my dream, I sat at a table, and I was looking at this dessert on a plate in front of me. The clarity of this dream was amazing; I had full, sensory overload. I saw every aspect of this recipe, and I am certain I had the ability of taste. The strangest part of this dream/recipe, is that it had a name. There is no arguing the logic of a dreaming mind. I remembered the name when I awoke, and I immediately jotted down everything before the memory escaped me.

This recipe was prepared for me by Sherry Miller. When she made it for me, I salivated at the sight of this sinfully delicious dessert.

**SERVES 12**

Two 30-ounce rolls chocolate chip cookie dough, any brand
(if you are fierce, you could make it from scratch, but I don't
have those instructions)
One 15-ounce jar peanut butter of your liking, room temperature
(I suggest creamy)
1 quart chocolate ice cream
1 quart vanilla ice cream
1 cup milk
1 container chocolate Magic Shell

Spread the chocolate chip cookie dough over the bottom of two 9 x 13-inch foil lasagna pans, using a small spatula, and make it about ⅓-inch thick. You can figure out the depth by sticking your finger in it. Make sure you don't eat all the cookie dough first. Bake according to the instructions on the package.

When the cookie sheets are done, and have cooled, set them aside. Spread a layer of peanut butter on one of the cookie sheets in the pan, about ⅓-inch thick.

✦✦✦✦✦✦✦✦✦✦✦✦✦✦✦✦✦✦✦✦✦✦✦✦✦✦✦✦✦✦✦✦✦✦✦✦✦✦✦✦✦✦✦✦✦

The following procedures need to be done rather quickly, due to the nature of the ingredients: Take your chocolate ice cream, and put a few huge scoops in a mixing bowl, add up to half of the milk gradually, just enough to help soften the ice cream, and mix. Spread the softened ice cream on top of the layer of peanut butter.

Take the second cookie sheet, gently remove it from the pan, and place it on top of the chocolate ice cream layer.

Soften the vanilla ice cream, just like the chocolate ice cream step. Make a layer on top of the new cookie sheet, about ⅓-inch thick. Yes, it has got to be thick.

Pour Magic Shell all over the layer of vanilla ice cream. Smother it like a doting mother. You want it to be completely covered. At this point, you should have a total of six layers, which is technically a "lasagna-style" presentation.

Place the Vancouver Lasagna in the freezer. When the dessert has chilled for at least 4 hours, cut it just like lasagna. This should feed several people at one sitting, or one person at several sittings (not including munchie attacks).

Side effects may include tooth decay, rapid weight gain, sugar overload, taste bud shock, and brainfreeze.

Not recommended to those with diabetes, lactose intolerance, and/or allergic reactions to peanuts and peanut butter.

In case of emergency, please consult a professional physician.

# STAR COOKIES AND NO-BAKE COOKIES

## David Ellefson, *Megadeth*

**E**ver since I was a kid I always look forward to two things: cookies and Christmas. So it's no surprise that my culinary skills always lead me back to baking, especially when the holiday season rolls around. Both of these cookie recipes work great during the holidays, especially if you can take a vacation from your rock star low-carb diet for a few days. I recommend serving these with a strong cup of Starbucks Caffe Verona or French-pressed French Roast blend. They will work well with your favorite 'nog, too. The caffeine and sugar are a surefire way to get the creative juices flowing as you ring out the old year and start rockin' in the New Year. Don't forget the mistletoe and enjoy!

## STAR COOKIES

**MAKES 6 TO 7 DOZEN COOKIES**

| | |
|---|---|
| ½ pound (2 sticks) butter | 2 teaspoons baking soda |
| 1 cup raw sugar | 2 teaspoons vanilla extract |
| 1 cup brown sugar | 3 cups all-purpose flour |
| 1 cup peanut butter | Granulated white sugar, for rolling |
| 1 teaspoon salt | Brach's Stars |
| 2 large eggs | |

Preheat the oven to 350°F.

Cream together the butter, sugars, and peanut butter. Stir in the salt, eggs, baking soda, vanilla, and flour. Form the mixture into small balls and roll lightly in white sugar. Place each ball on a baking sheet, about 1 inch apart, and bake for 8 minutes.

Remove from the oven and place a Brach's chocolate star on each cookie. Place back in the oven for no more than 2 minutes, to slightly melt the stars onto the cookies. Remove from the oven, place on a cooling rack, and serve warm and gooey. Delicious!

♦♦♦♦♦♦♦♦♦♦♦♦♦♦♦♦♦♦♦♦♦♦♦♦♦♦♦♦♦♦♦♦♦♦♦♦♦♦♦♦♦♦♦♦

## NO-BAKE COOKIES

**MAKES 5 TO 6 DOZEN COOKIES**

4 tablespoons (½ stick) butter

½ cup milk

2 cups sugar

3 tablespoons unsweetened cocoa

½ cup peanut butter

2 cups oatmeal

Combine the butter, milk, sugar, and cocoa in a saucepan. Bring to a boil and cook for 2 minutes. Remove from the heat and stir in the peanut butter and oatmeal.

Drop tablespoon-size lumps of mixture onto wax paper and let cool. Ready to eat within minutes!

What's great about these cookies is that they don't require any baking. So even if you have a tendency to burn water while cooking, you at least have a shot at doing these up right.

◆◆◆◆◆◆◆◆◆◆◆◆◆◆◆◆◆◆◆◆◆◆◆◆◆◆◆◆◆◆◆◆◆◆◆◆◆◆◆◆◆◆◆◆◆◆◆◆◆◆◆◆

# BETTER THAN SEXXX

## Ivan L. Moody, *Five Finger Death Punch*

**B**eing on the road most of the year, I rarely get the luxury of enjoying a home-cooked meal. So when I do have the opportunity to indulge, there are definitely a couple faves that I insist on having. One of which is a dessert my parents used to make when I was young. Usually it was a special occasion when it was prepared (like not getting kicked out of school, or no complaints from the neighbors for putting gas on their lawns). So I figured that this particular recipe would be stellar to share with all you monster-size, munchies-cravin' knuckleheads. This an easy recipe, and it's guaranteed to satisfy even the pickiest of dessert freaks. I hope you enjoy it as much as I do.

**SERVES 8**

An ass load of graham crackers
Two 3.4-ounce packages Jell-O French Vanilla instant pudding
3½ cups cold milk
Homemade Chocolate Frosting (recipe follows)
One 8-ounce tub whipped topping (optional)

Line 9 x 13–inch baking pan with whole graham crackers.

Mix the pudding with the milk according to package directions. Pour half of the pudding over the graham crackers and smooth the top.

Add a second layer of graham crackers. Add a second layer of pudding and smooth the top. Add a final layer of graham crackers. Smooth the homemade chocolate frosting over that last layer of graham crackers.

Cover the baking pan and let sit in the refrigerator for 24 hours. It needs time to set, so be patient.

Serve chilled with or without whipped topping on top.

Love and Respect

## HOMEMADE CHOCOLATE FROSTING

**3 tablespoons butter**
**3 tablespoons milk**
**2 tablespoons light corn syrup**
**1 teaspoon vanilla extract**
**2 squares (2 ounces) unsweetened chocolate, chopped**
**1½ cups confectioners' sugar**

Bring butter, milk, and corn syrup to a boil in a saucepan, and remove from the heat. Add vanilla, two chocolate squares, and powdered sugar. Mix well.

# WACKY CAKE WITH WHIPPED CHOCOLATE GANACHE AND PECAN PENUCHE TOPPING

## Morgan Lander, *Kittie*

Since my birth some twenty-seven years ago, I have been on the hunt for something divine. I have scoured the globe in hopes of discovering something undoubtedly pure and as close to the real thing as possible. The Holy Grail of baking, that inner "piece" that so many speak of. This life of deprivation has taken its toll. Every missed birthday treat? Wedding? Bake sale? Dessert bar visit or glare through a window at a pastry shop? A slap in the face! It has made my life almost unbearable and in a way forced me down a treacherous path in search of alternatives and the perfect substitute.

I am talking about cake here, people.

You see, I am allergic to eggs, which makes baking very difficult. Things just don't seem to stick together and work out without them, which has led me on this unfulfilled journey of cake discovery. Until now!

This recipe is an amalgamation of a traditional "wacky" or "war-time" cake—which was created during times when essentials like eggs and milk were harder to come by, or were rationed—and what is essentially a fudge recipe. The ganache is there to help the fudge stay on top of the cake, but it doesn't hurt that it's yummy. This cake is decadent, moist, light and fluffy, everything a cake should be, including delicious . . . just without the eggs!

### WACKY CAKE

1½ cups all-purpose flour

1 cup granulated sugar

¼ cup unsweetened cocoa

1 teaspoon baking soda

½ teaspoon salt

6 tablespoons vegetable oil

1 tablespoon distilled white vinegar

1 teaspoon vanilla extract

1 cup cold water

◆◆◆◆◆◆◆◆◆◆◆◆◆◆◆◆◆◆◆◆◆◆◆◆◆◆◆◆◆◆◆◆◆◆◆◆◆◆◆◆◆◆◆◆◆◆◆

**GANACHE**

1 pound good dark chocolate, such as Lindt or Merckens

1 cup heavy cream

**PECAN PENUCHE**

3 tablespoons butter

¾ cup firmly packed brown sugar

¼ cup heavy cream

1 teaspoon vanilla

¾ cup confectioners' sugar

1 cup pecans or nut of your choice

Butter a 9-inch cake pan and dust lightly with flour. Preheat the oven to 350°F.

Sift the flour, granulated sugar, cocoa, baking soda, and salt into a medium bowl. In a separate, smaller bowl, mix the oil, vinegar, vanilla, and cold water. Pour over the ingredients. Blend with rubber spatula or fork until well mixed. Pour into the prepared pan.

Bake for 30 minutes. Remove from oven and cool.

To make the ganache chop the chocolate into small pieces. In a heavy saucepan, heat the cream over medium-high heat, stirring frequently, until it just starts to boil. Remove from heat and add the chocolate. Stir until chocolate is completely melted and texture is smooth. Let cool completely.

In an electric mixer, whip the ganache until it is stiff and the consistency of whipped cream. Note: As an alternative, you could opt not to whip the ganache, which will result in a shiny, chocolate glaze that can be poured and spread onto the cake.

Frost the cooled cake.

Toast the nuts for the penuche in dry skillet over medium heat until they turn slightly brown. Set aside to cool, then chop.

Melt the butter in a heavy medium saucepan. Add the brown sugar and stir in the cream and vanilla. Boil over low heat for 2 minutes, stirring constantly. Remove from heat and stir in the confectioners' sugar and the nuts. Spread quickly over the top of the cake. Ganache will melt slightly.

+++++++++++++++++++++++++++++++++++++++++++++++++++++++

# AJETTA MISSISSIPPI MUD CAKE

## Michael Wilton, *Queensrÿche*

**T**he Mississippi Mud Cake is a fourth-generation recipe that began in the Deep South with my wife's family. It has moved up to the Northwest and is now a sweet-tooth favorite in my family. One of the sweetest cakes of all time, this dessert should be dosed in small portions. I prefer it with a cup of freshly brewed black coffee.

SERVES 12

### CAKE

1 cup (2 sticks) butter, at room temperature

2 cups sugar

1/3 cup unsweetened cocoa

4 large eggs

1½ cups all-purpose flour

½ teaspoon baking powder

1 cup flaked coconut

1 cup chopped pecans

One 6-ounce jar marshmallow creme

### ICING

8 tablespoons (1 stick) butter

1/3 cup unsweetened cocoa

One 1-pound box confectioners' sugar

1 teaspoon vanilla extract

One 5-ounce can evaporated milk

Preheat the oven to 350°F.

Whip the butter until creamy, then beat in the sugar and cocoa. Add the eggs, 1 at a time. Add the flour and baking powder and mix until smooth. Fold the coconut and pecans into the mixture.

Pour batter into 13 x 9-inch pan and bake for 30 minutes. Remove from the oven and spread the jar of marshmallow creme over the hot cake. Let cake cool in pan.

Meanwhile to make the icing, mix together all ingredients and only enough of the evaporated milk to make the icing smooth and spreadable.

Ice the cake once it has cooled down.

# ACKN⊕WLEDGMENTS

There are a ton of people I must thank for helping me put this rockin' book together: Lisa "The Rock & Roll Outlaw" Seabury; Allison "Not Another Beer Lunch" Villareal; Alexandra "The Final Cut Pro" Joe; Amy "I Hope the Phillies Win a World Series Soon" Sciarretto; Andrew "I'm Too Metal" Sheed; Anthony "My Ears Ache" Guzzardo; Antonio "Run to the Hills" Marsillo; Bill "Rocken Like Dokken" Meis; Bryan "For Whom the Bell Tolls" Mechutan; Charley "Have You Ever Heard of Metallica" Siegel; Chris "You Want Hot Sauce" Caffery; Chris "Lock Up Your Daughters" Pacifico; Chris "Get Chopped" Santos; Christine "The Tax Women" Scarnici; Dan "I'm Not Driving" Rozenblum; Dana "Horns High" Strutz; Darren "Metal Up Your Ass" Edwards; Dave "Get to the Chopper" Ardolina; Dave "Caught in a Mosh" Brenner; Dave "My Glasses Are Bigger than Yours" Turner; David "Whiplash" Brown; Denise "The Video Ninja" Korycki; Dennis "On a Steel Horse I Ride" Clapp; Don "I Suck at John Madden" Mroczko; Don "Hail & Kill" Robertson; Dov "The NY Mets Rule" Teta; Duncan "Newcastle Rocks" Hutchison; Eric "Holy Diver" Collins; Eric "Pounding Metal" Lemasters; George "Mike Piazza Is the Greatest Player Ever" Dewey; George "Stand Up & Shout" Vallee; Garrett "Another Bottle of Jack" Robinson; Glenn "Cook Out with Your Book Out" Hillman; Ian "F'ing Seabreeze" Wright; Jamie "Bite the Bullet" Roberts; Jason "Cowboys from Hell" Lekberg; Jean "For Those About to Rock" Sagendorph; Jeanne "I Love Metal" Drewson; Jeff "Man O' War Rules" Gershener; Jim "Walk" Pate; Jon "Ratt & Roll" Bomser; Jon "Who Is Better than Chris Squire" Freeman; John "WASP Rules" McDonald; John "Wendy's Anyone?" Conley; John "I Want to Move to Antarctica" Alia; Kelli "Bullet Belts" Malella; Kervans "I Could Do Voiceovers" Barthelemy; Kevin "Shout at the Devil" Strang; Leo "The Heavy Metal Santa" Lavoro; Liz "I Love Blast Beats" Ciavarella; Liz "Tones of Death" Snair; Loana "Denim & Leather" Valencia; Luke "I Want a Bison Burger" Tobias; Marc "Bacon Anyone" Schapiro; Mary "You Can't Get More Metal than the Steelers" Wickson;

Melissa "Heavy Metal Cookies" Musso; Missi "Dave Lombardo Is God" Callazzo; Mitch "The King of Metal" Lafon; Munsey "I Love Pizza" Ricci; Nathan "Madison Square Garden" McFall; Nick "What's Wrong with Phil Collins?" Tieder; Pat "I Wanna Rock" Egan; Paul "Kicking Ass and Taking Names" Dippolito; Pete "Drunken Monkey" Tsakiris; Rachel "Eat the Rich" Bostic; Randy "The Closet Met Fan" Derebegian; Rev. Dave "Grill It Up" Ciancio; Rob "Running with the Devil" Gill; Rob "Doom On" Goodman; Sarah "Scream for Me, Long Beach" Branham; Sean "I Will Kick Your Ass in Darts" Campbell; Summer "Summer Sault" Lacy; Scott "Another Shot of Jäger" Givens; Shawn "Your Excuses Are Your Own" Quinn; and Tim "Girls, Girls, Girls" Yasui.

To my entire family; all of the bands; managers; record companies; and the entire Atria / Simon & Schuster family—thanks for making this dream come true. The music of Moth Eater; Aria Pro 2 Bass Guitars; Orange Amps; The Music Cartel; the Brothers & Sisters of METAL of the In Transition Alliance of KOC; the New England, Pennsylvania, and New York chapters of the Tearjerkers; all the cool people who work at record stores and don't ask you "You want to buy a dishwasher with your CD?"; college radio stations; magazines; blogs and websites that continue supporting the greatest style of music; my friends who have let me pass out on their floor; promoters who hook up the bands with gas money; people who support the arts and don't steal music; spicy food; ice-cold beer; and Loud Fucking Music! This book is for you. Beers Up!

# INDEX